TALES FROM THE
SAN DIEGO CHARGERS
SIDELINE

TALES FROM THE
SAN DIEGO CHARGERS
SIDELINE

A COLLECTION OF THE GREATEST CHARGERS STORIES EVER TOLD

SID BROOKS
WITH GERRI BROOKS

FOREWORD BY
DAN FOUTS

SPORTS
PUBLISHING

Sports Publishing books may be purchased in bulk at special discounts for sales promotion, corporate gifts, fund-raising, or educational purposes. Special editions can also be created to specifications. For details, contact the Special Sales Department, Sports Publishing, 307 West 36th Street, 11th Floor, New York, NY 10018 or sportspubbooks@skyhorsepublishing.com.

Sports Publishing® is a registered trademark of Skyhorse Publishing, Inc.®, a Delaware corporation.

Visit our website at www.sportspubbooks.com.

10 9 8 7 6 5 4 3 2 1

Library of Congress Cataloging-in-Publication Data is available on file.

Series design by Tom Lau
Cover photo credit AP Images

ISBN: 978-1-61321-716-0
Ebook ISBN: 978-1-61321-749-8

Printed in the United States of America

Contents

Foreword

By Dan Fouts

For Eric Seivers, our rookie tight end in 1981, it was his first "End of Training Camp/Birthday Party for Louie Kelcher and Billy Shields" celebration. So when he pushed Sid "Doc" Brooks into the deep end of the swimming pool, he didn't know that Doc couldn't swim. As cheers and laughter erupted and Doc floundered, I did the only thing I could do. Seeing only Doc's eyeballs breaking the surface of the water, I jumped in, clothes on and all.

I got Doc to the side of the pool, directly under the diving board and tried to calm him as best I could. "Doc, the good news is I saved your life…the bad news is you owe me your life!"

That is what any friend would do, especially for a man whose world was jammed full of friends. And that is what this book is about more than anything—friends.

A locker room is a unique, mysterious, and wonderful place. Its doors are open to only a select few. What goes on there is known only to the members of the team, but what is remembered lasts a lifetime. Sidney Joseph Patrick Brooks, AKA "The Doc," not only was our equipment manager, he was our counselor, our collaborator, our domino partner, our critic and cheerleader, and most importantly, our friend.

"Mr. Brooks, I can't go out to practice in this helmet, it doesn't have a face mask," I protested. I couldn't believe this, my first practice in the National Football League with the San Diego Chargers and this guy gives me a helmet without a face mask! The year was 1973; the Chargers had just hired a new equipment man (Doc), and drafted a new quarterback in the third round (me). Thus began a relationship that has lasted over three decades.

In my 15 years with the Chargers and with Doc, there were many changes—five head coaches, at least as many general managers, hundreds of players, heck, even two owners. The constant, though, was Doc. As players, we could always count on seeing Doc bright and early, every morning, all year long in the locker room. He always boasted a smile and a quip; nothing went unnoticed by him.

Doc's job was more than handing out sweats, socks, and jocks. He was always on the lookout for opportunities for us as players to help out in the San Diego community. Whether it was a bowling or golf tournament, visits to children in local hospitals at Christmas, blood drives, or flights with the Blue Angels, Doc was always at the forefront when it came to supporting the community. He helped the players improve their public profile, and learn what it meant to give back to the community.

From a dedicated and decorated career in the United States Air Force to being the first African-American equipment manager in the NFL to being a devoted husband and father, Doc's career and life have been full and satisfying. Through it all, he has enriched the lives of countless others. Reading his book will give you an inside look at this part of his life and the lives of those who were fortunate enough to call him a friend.

Enjoy!

Introduction

In the glamorous game of football, there are stars that shine on the field: the acclaimed football players and coaches, men whose names are uttered in awe and sometimes defended with swear words and fists. In the front offices, the owners and general managers are touted for putting together the big entertainment picture for game day. But behind the glitz and glory, there are the little men who keep the show on the road. They make sure the players hit the field as ready warriors in fine regalia from shiny helmets to flashy shoes. For twenty-seven years Sidney J. (Doc) Brooks, the equipment manager for the San Diego Chargers, was privileged to be one of the little men who made sure on game day his team was ready to dazzle.

The San Diego Chargers football team and the NFL were an entirely different world from the one Sid was familiar with and a long way from Saint Genevieve, Missouri, the town he grew up in with his father and his two brothers. His father, whom he was fortunate to have until he reached the ripe old age of ninety-five, reared his brothers and him alone. Sid was six years old when his mother died from a head injury following a car crash. He had no memory of her. His father never spoke of her. Sid spoke of emptiness in himself because of her absence that haunted him all his life. He was an adult when he gathered bits and pieces of information about her and learned that from a family of twelve siblings, she worked her way through college and was on her way to her teaching job when a car crash took her life. He knew then that he had to make something of his life. Sid joined the Air Force, where he learned discipline and the rewards of dedication and hard work. He credited the loving care his father took of him and his brothers without help and the fighting spirit of his mother for the drive in him, a drive that led him to give his best in both of his careers.

As a kid, Sid never saw a football game up close. Very few black families lived in his home town, so he rode a bus fifty-five miles to a segregated high school. When his high school team played their football games, he was riding the bus home. He was not permitted inside the Ste. Genevieve High School stadium for a school function, so he watched the local high school games through the trees surrounding the football field. He was nineteen and in the Air Force when he attended his first live football game. Army played Air Force in Misawa Air Base, Japan. Sid saw his first professional football game September 21, 1962 while stationed in New York City. The New York Giants beat the Detroit Lions 17 to 14. He thought then that was as close as he would ever get to a professional football player.

But by working hard and preparing for opportunity, Sid was ready when his chance came in the form of an announcement in the sports section of the Colorado Springs *Gazette*. A professional team needed an equipment manager. He hesitated, but only briefly. He'd been told that opportunity only knocks once, so he took the offer when the San Diego Chargers presented him a job as the equipment manager for the team. When Sid began his career with the Chargers, the NFL was fifty-three years old. It would be another twenty years before a different team hired an African American equipment manager.

Sid was thirty-eight when he began his job as equipment manager with the Chargers, a career that would have made him a laughing stock in his hometown had he dreamed it out loud as a boy. No one he knew would have believed the possibility. Growing up, he hadn't known that such a position existed. Anything to do with football was far removed from any aspirations he had for himself. Given the chance, he did it his way. His way was enough to endear him to the entire National Football League for as long as he was a part of the league and to this day.

The basement in Qualcomm Stadium is where the Chargers equipment is kept. It was the San Diego Stadium in 1973 when Sid first set foot in the 54,542-seat football arena. This arena was a concrete bowl where the echoes of thousands of cheering fans gave him goose-bumps and filled him with awe. The basement, where the equipment department and trainers, known as dungeon rats, ruled the locker room, is where he became caretaker for all who crossed the threshold. Within those walls resided the pungent, sweaty smell of victory and the taste of stinging gall in defeat. In the mornings before the arrival of the gridiron warriors, the lockers stood empty except for the gear; shoes lined up, helmets shined and waiting, shoulder pads on the shelves, and jerseys hanging ready, as though the first sergeant would come through for inspection. Left over from his Air Force days, he assured that there was an air of military correctness and pride in the personification of that room. He hoped that readiness was a reflection of who he was. Names that changed over the years shouted in all their glory above the lockers. Some of those names, many of which will appear throughout the book, caused the breath to catch in his throat, and the thrill of their talent to astound him.

It would be dark, quiet, and damp before the coffee and doughnuts, before the cheerfulness and the brooding, before the arrogant swaggers and the fearful hopefulness, before the boom boxes, high-fives, back-slapping, and the sound of dominos brought the locker room to life. The veterans were there to offer Sid advice on how to survive in the NFL. He was sought out, not just for football equipment, but also for special needs: marital problems, financial advice, where to eat, where to buy furniture, how to make a difference in the community with charitable contributions, and advice to the lovelorn. But he'd prepared for the requests, aware of the ones who needed him most. Some were still boys, you know. It was not only for the equipment that they sought him out; that had been made ready. He was and always will be know as the domino doctor, "Doc," champion domino player as he has been affectionately named throughout the league. Some that boarded the elevator to B2, the basement, and came through the doors of the locker room schemed to steal the Doc's crown at the domino table. These stories provide the opportunity to watch the doctor and an array of challengers in action while playing games other than football. Camaraderie, not seen any place else outside the locker room, except maybe on a military battlefield, existed in abundance in the pranks they played on one another. These pranks were not only intended to lift spirits, but measured one's ability to withstand adversity, created a feeling of family, and brought the team closer.

What is about to be revealed in these pages is the truth, the whole truth, and nothing but the truth so help me. Much of what's contained here began more than thirty years ago, but time did not erase Sid's memory. His locker room days made a lasting impression on him and all who came in contact with him. There are witnesses that will swear to his most flabbergasting stories. One such person, on whom he made a lasting impression, is Dan Fouts.

Dan Fouts has added to Sid's domino tales "The Sid Brooks Rule." The rule is as follows:

"I played dominoes with Sid a lot of years. The Sid Brooks rule came about because Sid was either A) a bad cheater; or B) couldn't count. When Sid and I played dominoes and used all my dominoes to win a hand, the normal procedure is that the opponent's dominoes left in his hand would be counted and the number added to the winner's total.

"Sid would often have a fist full of bones in his hands, blurt out a number at random, and throw his bones face down into the bone yard. I was quick enough one day to stop the bones before they landed in the pile and counted the spots. They were way, way over what he'd blurted out, shorting me points I should have earned. Therefore the Sid Brooks Rule was put into place, which allows a player to throw his bones in face down and say whatever number he wants. But if that number is challenged, and he is wrong, the real number plus ten more points would be added to the winner's score. If he was right and he was challenged, the player who had won the hand would lose ten points.

"The Sid Brooks Rule has added a bit of suspense and a lot of laughs to the game of dominoes whenever my friends and I play. And in thinking about Sid, as I often do, I would say that he probably wasn't really a cheater, or that he couldn't count, [but rather] he was just messing with us and being Doc."

—Gerri Brooks, 2014

No names have been changed
to protect the innocent; there are no innocents.
All of the accused are guilty as charged.

— The Doc

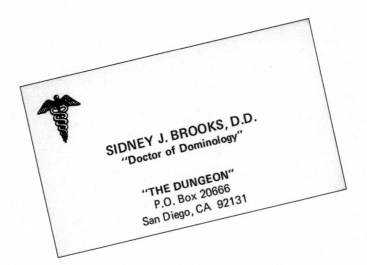

SIDNEY J. BROOKS, D.D.
"Doctor of Dominology"

"THE DUNGEON"
P.O. Box 20666
San Diego, CA 92131

TALES FROM THE

SAN DIEGO CHARGERS

SIDELINE

1

JOINING THE BOLTS

My secretary, Scotty Cullitan, laid the sports section of the Colorado Springs *Gazette* across her desk at the Air Force Academy. "Look at this article, Sid," she said. "The San Diego Chargers are looking for an equipment manager. Why don't you apply?"

I bent over her shoulder and read the article. "I'm not an equipment manager," I said. By January of 1973, I was eligible to retire after serving 20 years in the Air Force. A career in civilian life was on my mind. My job title then—Non-Commissioned Officer in charge of the Air Force Academy Cadet Athletic Supply Branch, Facilities and Support Division—had nothing to do with being an equipment manager. Everything I did in that role involved a paper transaction. The actual uniform, and what to do with it, were different challenges; I hadn't suited out one athlete, even though I knew the job requirements.

I backed away from Scotty shaking my head. "I don't even know how to put a face mask on a helmet." I believed my chance of landing a job in the NFL was nil to none, and refused to dwell on it.

"If you can persuade an Air Force Major not to argue with you until he becomes a Bird Colonel—and get away with it—then you can handle a bunch of athletes and coaches," Scotty insisted. "You're right for that job." She sent my resume to the Chargers in spite of my protests. Three days later, I was aboard a plane on its way to San Diego for an interview after receiving a phone call from Bob Hood, then an executive assistant with the Chargers.

Somebody's Watching Me

Bob Hood—a 20-something, white, seventies rebel, with long dark hair that covered his ears and a fu-Manchu mustache—picked me up from the Stardust Hotel, where the Chargers had put me up the night before. Hood drove me to what was then called San Diego Stadium for a meeting with Harland Svare, the Chargers head coach and general manager. I felt like a starving actor about to be discovered by a big Hollywood producer. Like everyone on the outside imagining what it's like in a place where the stars shine, the lure of the NFL was glamorous. I was thrilled at the prospect of sharing in the exciting allure.

As I sat across from Harland's desk for the first interview of my life, I clutched my hands in my lap. Joining the Air Force 20 years prior had been a simple act of answering a few questions on paper and signing on the dotted line. This time I didn't know what to expect. Why I'd let Scotty talk me into chasing this impossible dream job, I couldn't remember. Harland appeared friendly—a young, smiling, blue-eyed blond with a firm handshake.

Behind Harland, a door stood open a crack, providing a tiny glimpse into a dark immeasurable space. Without any familiarity with the building, I didn't know whether the door led to another room or a hallway, but shadows passed back and forth with regularity. Every few minutes I caught a glimpse of what appeared to be a face and a set of eyes peering through the opening, and an eerie feeling that I was being watched enveloped me. I noticed that neither Bob nor Harland appeared to notice the movement behind the door. Each time I answered a question, a shadow moved away, then another came into view. I tried focusing on Harland and the questions he asked while making surreptitious glances toward whoever it was in the shadows that was observing me.

On my way out of town after my brief visit, I thought I'd seen beautiful San Diego for the last time; I thought I had little hope of landing the job. It was not that I didn't think that I'd made a good impression. But rather Bob told me that since posting the position, the Chargers had received four hundred applications for the job. With that in mind, I still considered my visit a success, as I imagined any sports fan would upon being granted temporary access into the world of the NFL. The evening before my interview, Bob and I had dinner at Bully's, a Mission Valley steak house patronized by sports figures and enthusiasts. I met Mike Garrett, Heisman Trophy winner out of USC, All-American, and one of the leading rushers in the NFL. I was returning home to tell my sons that I had shaken the hand of a premier football player. (As it turns out, Mike Garrett became one of my lifelong friends.)

Years later, Deacon told me that Harland had stationed three black men from the Chargers' roster—Willie Wood, a defensive back coach; Deacon Jones, a defensive lineman; and Bob Moorman, a scout—behind the door to spy on my interview, monitor the way I answered questions, and measure how I held up under pressure.

"You better have looked good, or we would have run your butt out of San Diego. You were coming in here representing us brothers, and you had to do us proud," Deacon told me sometime later.

Equipment Managing 101

The Chargers wanted me in San Diego ASAP. Their 1973 spring mini camp was about to begin without an equipment manager on board.

I called Larry Elliott, the equipment manager for the Denver Broncos, to tell him that I'd been hired by the Chargers and to ask if he'd be willing to give me a crash course in the fundamentals of football equipment management. I had met him once when a very bad snowstorm forced the Broncos to move their practice to the Academy's indoor facility. He agreed, and that weekend, on my two days off, Larry walked me through Equipment Managing 101. I crammed like a failing student the night before final exams. My head felt swollen from soaking up so many of the NFL's official rules.

When I left Larry that weekend, I still didn't know how to secure facemasks on helmets, fit and repair shoulder pads, or fasten and remove cleats. Back at the Academy, I worked from early morning until late at night with the equipment managers in the athletic department, going over what Larry hadn't had time to teach me. A week later, I took vacation time and went to San Diego for my first mini camp. I was still signed up for four years with the Air Force, and that big obstacle weighed heavily on my mind. While I was away from the Air Force Academy, Colonel Frank Merritt, the athletic director and a former lineman at West Point, convinced the Academy's Superintendent to pull strings to get me discharged. "I want you to learn how to be a civilian," he told me. I became an official San Diego Charger. From that moment on, I wore lightning bolts, and when I mentioned the Chargers, I said "we" as in, "We have a game on Sunday." I was part of the "we" that was the Chargers.

The Locker Room

The sign outside the door read, "Authorized personnel only per the Commissioner, Pete Rozelle." Reading that, my butt tightened up so much that you couldn't pull a silk thread through it. The locker room was where football players were most apt to relax and let you in on their vulnerabilities. It housed the equipment room and training room, and was located on level two of the basement of San Diego Stadium—or "B2," as the guys who worked there called it. Although the team has since moved their general offices and facility to a building on Murphy Canyon Road, the Chargers still use that locker room on home game days. My office for many of my 27 years was just inside the locker room. To the left of that office was the equipment room, with rows and rows of shelves that held a multimillion-dollar inventory of equipment. The equipment issue window, where players and coaches came for socks, jocks, T-shirts, and shorts, opened to the locker room. On the opposite end of the equipment room, behind doors that separated it from the locker room, was the training room. The basement was ruled by those affectionately called "dungeon rats," the equipment department staff and trainers.

9449 Friars Road, Apt. B2

I couldn't write about the Chargers' locker room without mentioning Bronco Hinek. I arrived at the Chargers' locker room for my first day of work at 4:30 a.m. and found my newly appointed, round-faced, long-haired, 22-year-old assistant equipment manager, Bronco, waiting for me. "Didn't have to fight the traffic," he said, and laughed, as though he had a secret.

"This is the way it is, Sid," he said when he introduced me to the innerworkings of a NFL equipment department. "Let the players think they're in charge, but know that you are."

During the off-season, Bronco resided in the Bay Area. But while in San Diego, he told me that his address was 9449 Friars Road, Apt. B2. "Beats paying rent," he said, grinning. But I was not in on the joke.

Bronco had been a part-time assistant for the previous four seasons, and he knew his way around the equipment room. I followed him around the locker room, learning the system. Later that day I picked up the equipment manager's mail, and noticed that it had the same address that Bronco had given me earlier— the stadium address. "B2," of course, was the basement of San Diego Stadium. I almost doubled over from laughing so hard. Bronco slept that whole preseason in the locker room.

Camp Site

Bronco and I prepared for the mini-camp held in the open field at the southeast end of the Stardust Hotel golf course on Friars Road. In those days one stoplight controlled the flow of traffic between the stadium and the practice field. Travel time from the stadium to the Stardust took approximately ten to 12 minutes by car. Bronco and I turned the golf course into a football field, set up goal posts, painted 10-yard lines, and arranged to have all the bags and the sleds (large, overstuffed, stabilized, punching bags used to practice blocking) brought to the field from storage. That's how it started. Then the fun began.

Lining the field was as foreign to me as the Greek language. I didn't realize how precisely accurate the lines had to be. The first time I tried to paint 10-yard markers on the field, my line resembled Lombard Street in San Francisco, the most crooked street in the world. Bronco lay on the grass, laughing out loud while holding his side and gasping for breath. My next attempt looked like the tire tracks my nearly blind grandmother made after backing up her car without her glasses on, and I joined Bronco in laughter. My young assistant was already a pro at the outside stuff, and I watched him square off lines with the accuracy of a carpenter. Every millimeter of an inch was accounted for, which made sense since accurate yards determine the outcome of any given game. Knowing that this particular part of the job was not meant for me, I let Bronco take over when it came to lining the field. They didn't call me the equipment *manager* for nothing.

2

MINI-CAMP

Johnny Rodgers

Orientation for mini-camp began when the doors to the locker room opened. Draftees, free agents, convalescents, and veterans acquired through trade poured in to begin their indoctrination into the Chargers' program. Only players new to the team and those recovering from injuries were required to report on opening day.

I was familiar with many of the names on the Chargers roster from watching college football games, and I tried, in the short time I had to prepare, to familiarize myself with some of the faces. My first day I was as uncertain as an intern performing surgery for the first time—all clumsy fingers and shaky hands. I thought it would seem professional if I knew a little bit about each of the new guys, including the draftees. But the first player on the scene that season proved my research unnecessary. Johnny Rodgers let everyone know exactly who he thought he was.

"J.R. The Super Star," he announced out loud, head in the air and not blinking an eye. I managed to hold back a snicker and keep my face blank. I knew who he was; with hands like clutches, he could run the 40-yard dash in four seconds flat.

"Johnny Rodgers, Heisman Trophy winner," he said and stuck his chest out, as though waiting for me to bow. He waved a plastic doll-like figure modeled after him and sporting his number 20 on its helmet and jersey. I didn't bow, but replaced his halo with a Chargers helmet and went about preparing to outfit the rest of the team. More players poured in, and I got busy. Before long, hoots and hollers broke out behind me. I glanced up from fitting one of the other players and spotted Johnny Rodgers passing out J.R. Super Star buttons to the other players. The stars had shot right out of the sky and landed in the locker room. It was obvious that all of the attention he had received from the Heisman had gone to his head, and no one blamed him. The Heisman was an honor few athletes experienced.

Johnny pranced as if he were ready to make believers out of us—and then he did. On the first play of his initial game for the Chargers, he returned the ball back on kickoff for a touchdown. He was so excited that he came back to the sideline rubbing his legs together, announcing that he was about to wet himself. After being told there was nowhere to go to the bathroom on the sideline, he crawled under a bench on his belly, and shielded by his teammates, he peed on the ground. His halo got wet, and his teammates didn't let him forget it.

Dan Fouts—The Rookie

I had already met Dan Fouts, the quarterback out of Oregon, prior to being selected by the Chargers in the third round of the 1973 draft. His college team had played Air Force in Colorado Springs the year before. Fouts came into the locker room and recognizing me, joked about breaking his school's passing record against the Air Force Academy.

"So what?" I said. "Throwing the ball in that high altitude is no big thing. Rocks fly in thin air."

Thus began the friendly banter between us, which has lasted to this day. Upon his arrival at Chargers' mini-camp, Fouts was a very young rookie, and I was an unsure and overwhelmed old rookie thrust headfirst into unknown territory. But we bonded well because both of us had found a familiar face.

I assigned numbers to players as they came in. Bronco had told me that it didn't matter much which number the players wore during mini-camp, so I issued numbers by availability—first come, first serve. Most players wanted to keep the numbers they'd worn through high school and college. I tried as best as I could to follow that pattern, wanting the guys to feel like we were trying to please them. When Dan Fouts arrived, number 11, his number in college, had been given to quarterback Tony Adams. I was nervous. I knew he would probably be the Chargers quarterback of the future, and I'd messed up already. In a state of uncertainty, I reached behind me, pulled an old discarded jersey from a box, and handed it to him, along with a helmet.

"This thing doesn't have a facemask," he said, examining the helmet.

I looked at the helmet in his hand and then at the facemasks lying in a box. I didn't know how to secure the facemask to the helmet, but I wasn't about to tell him that. "Just put the helmet on and go to practice," I told him. He has never let me forget that I sent him out to practice that first day without a face mask on his helmet.

His jersey on that first day was No. 18. But during the regular season, we agreed on No. 14, the number that appears on his jersey in the Hall of Fame today.

Gunter Enz

Gunter Enz, a soccer-style kicker from Vienna, Austria, was among the last to show up for mini-camp and pick up his equipment. American football was as much a novelty to him as he was to us. He spoke very little English and hesitated as though he wasn't sure he belonged. I knew how that felt. I was doing my best to get in the groove. I attempted to communicate with him by speaking louder, which made him laugh. It was clear that I wasn't the first English-speaking person to try that tactic with him. I laughed too, and in that way we communicated.

The Chargers had traveled throughout Europe searching for a kicker, and in Vienna they found their soccer-style, sidewinder kicker, who had been playing European football and studying to become a doctor. He had never kicked an American football before his try-out for the Chargers scouting party.

In the locker room, the long-haired 22-year-old was as skittish as a colt at the starting gate in Del Mar. This was his first introduction to the football gear worn in the NFL. Together we mastered the complete fitting of a football uniform with a lot of pointing and giggling. He learned which pieces went where, and how to put it on and take it off. He explained to me that a sidewinder kicker wore soccer shoes and kicked from the side of his foot, while kickers who kicked the ball straight-on used a square-toed kicking shoe.

Upon receiving his helmet, he stared at it as if we were preparing to send him into outer space. His face beamed with astonishment as Bronco attached a facemask with a one-bar, the type kickers use. After I applied his name on the front of his practice helmet, I told him to come in early the next day before practice so we could make sure everything fit correctly. Unlike the first player who showed up, he was humble, thanking me for the opportunity to play and admitting that he was unsure if he would fit in. He thanked everyone he saw that day within the first 24 hours as an equipment manager, I had witnessed unabashed arrogance and grateful humility. Nothing changed over the next 27 years, except the names.

Eugene V. Klein

Eugene Klein, the Chargers' owner when I began my 27 years with the team, was a large, powerful man, with a presence that overwhelmed. The day I met him I was so busy my tracks struggled to keep up with my shoes, and this big guy kept getting in the way and slowing me down. I assumed he was an agent for one of the players who had come to watch his investment, but he was all over the place, shaking the hand of one player after another. Simply put, I couldn't get anyone dressed with him around. I didn't want Coach Svare to get upset with me, so I went over to the big guy and said, "Excuse me, Sir, I'm trying to do a job here, and you're slowing up the players. I don't know who you are, but you can see them all when practice is over."

"I know who you are," he responded. "I'm Gene Klein. I read your resume, Sidney. The military trains good men." His smile saved me from the heart attack that I hoped would kill me on the spot. I thanked him for the opportunity to work for his team. "You earned it," he replied, raising his big hand to slap me on the back.

For the entire duration of the camp, he came to practice every day and addressed each of the veterans by name, and before the end of camp, he knew every new man on board at first glance. Dressed in jeans and a Chargers T-shirt, he made a point of speaking to all the staff and inquiring about their families with sincerity. After he met my wife he greeted her with a hug whenever he saw her, and laughed about me trying to throw him out of the locker room. A down to earth, regular guy, he told me once, "I love to eat hot dogs, popcorn, and chili when I'm in the stadium. Hell, it's a ballgame. That's what you're supposed to eat."

He was friendly and warm toward all the people on his staff. "We're family here," he said. And that's the way he made me feel throughout—and even after—his tenure with the Chargers. We remained in touch until his death. I am eternally grateful to him for making my family a part of his.

What's Good Enough for His Horses

I'd be negligent if I didn't share a tale or two about Gene Klein—or "EVK," as he was known throughout the league. He kept racehorses in Rancho Santa Fe. One of the horse trainers bought a new device to use on the racehorses called the "Pulsed

Magnetic Frequency Therapy Machine." Basically the thing was a group of large coils of copper wiring in the shape of a figure eight covered in electrician's tape. By creating a magnetic field around the horses' legs, the machine was suppose to increase the blood flow to that area, and thereby reduce swelling and remove waste. The end result was that the horses would recover quicker from their training. It seemed to work: several of the injured horses showed good results.

Excited about the effects the machine had on the horses, EVK thought, "Why not use it on the players, too?" The front office wanted the trainers—Larry Roberts, James Collins, Andy Myerson, and Lance Grugel—to begin using it on the players, and so they did. The horse trainers wouldn't give up the machine in the mornings, because they needed it for the ponies. So at noon, someone from the locker room would drive up to Rancho Santa Fe and borrow the machine.

The apparatus stunk of horse poop and urine, and was covered with horse hair. Even after it was cleaned the smell of the pouches was reminiscent of a stable. The big guys dubbed it "the horse machine." The trainers used the machine in conjunction with other treatments to treat sprains, strains, and bruises. Did it work? The players couldn't feel any effects from the machine while it was on, so the jokes began to fly. Some felt it didn't do anything, but one lineman said he really liked it because it made him "hung like a horse." Gary Johnson, a defensive lineman, had the best line. He said he felt like he had to whinny whenever the machine was on him.

A certain quarterback—whom I will not name because I owe him my life—felt a little put out that he had to wait for the horses' treatment before he could use the machine. "I've been up to the ranch," he said. "The barn for the horses is nicer than our locker room. EVK cares more about his horses than he does about us. If he really cared, he'd get us our own machine without the horse manure."

Use of the piece of equipment only lasted for one-half of the season, with no evidence that it made a difference. After the end of the season, we never saw it again. Like most treatment methods, if the boys believed it worked, then it worked. If not, then it didn't.

Gene Klein said there was a difference between his players and horses. The horses didn't have agents, so when they won, he collected the paycheck—and all he had to give the horses was food and water.

A Scare Before Practice

For my first practice of mini-camp in 1973, the new hopefuls showed up at the Stardust in practice gear, prancing, sprinting, and tossing the ball around while warming up. Gunter Enz, our new kicker, bounced a soccer ball off his head, his knees, and his feet like a happy little juggler while the rest of us watched his moves. The quarterbacks, Dan Fouts and Tony Adams, tossed balls back and forth to rookie receivers while waiting for the coaches to show up. All were ready to impress and make the team.

From the other side of the field some loud yelling erupted. I stared, along with everyone else, in the direction of the noise. I didn't know who the hecklers were until Bronco identified them. Veterans on the team: Jim Tolbert, Jeff Queen, Jeff Stag, Pete Barnes, Marty Domrest, Cid Edwards, Doug Wilkerson, Bryant Salter, and Deacon Jones made up the band creating the ruckus. They didn't come any closer, but Deacon, leading his traveling revival, yelled, "Rookies, listen up."

The new recruits got so quiet you could hear the blades of grass swaying. No one moved. Each one of us, including yours truly, was all ears.

"You better watch out, Rookies," Deacon yelled, backed by motions from the others. "You don't want no one-on-one with the Deac. I'll be out there tomorrow and put a move on you that'll make you wish you was home with your mama."

I stuck as close to Bronco as a shadow. "What's going on?" I asked.

"It's an indoctrination thing," Bronco told me. "The veterans are having fun with the new guys. Happens every year. They scare the crap out of the rookies because they can." He laughed. "You'll get used to them."

The laughter of the vets echoed as they walked away.

Deacon Jones—The Leader of the Pack and My Guardian, Too

Veteran players reported to mini-camp two days after the rookies came in. Deacon Jones' presence on the scene left no doubt that he was the voice of the team. I loved his straight-for-ward, loud-mouthed, no-nonsense gift of gab. Deacon called a team meeting, which didn't include me, but I snuck around a corner and eavesdropped just to hear him talk.

"Listen up, fellows," he told them while smoking a ciga-rette. "We have us a brother as the head equipment manager—first one in the league." He hung his head, as if in prayer, shook his head from side to side, and then looked up. "I just hope he don't f--k up. I can tell you this." He sucked in a lung full of smoke and shook his finger at the guys. Clouding their faces in an exhale of smoke, he said, "Nobody better f--k with him."

"I second the motion," Dave Costa said.

Hearing that, I was like James Brown. I felt good, but I knew my part in the deal; they could depend on me to deliver a well-run locker room. As Deacon had warned them not to, nobody messed with me.

A Tougher Look

During the summer, while we prepared for the season ahead, Harland asked Bob Hood and me to come up with a uniform that presented a more fearsome look than the baby-blue uniform and white helmet that was the Chargers' uniform at the time. He wanted it to look more like the Giants' dark blue. We went through some designs. Very few people know what Bob Hood and I went through to get someone to make the color changes on the helmet. We did a transparency to get the blue of the helmet to come through. Today the process is called reversing it out. In 1973 none of the sporting goods companies had the expertise to make it for us. We wanted to change the gray face mask that every team, from little league to the NFL, wore, but no one could make it for us. Riddell, from whom we bought the facemask, said they couldn't make it. We went to Dr. Dungard, a dentist, and he painted the face mask gold for us by coating them with a dental process. I hand painted the double and single bars on the face masks worn mainly by kickers and some receivers. The Chargers were the first team to wear a colored face mask, and all Bob and I received for our idea was an exclusive for one year. We told Riddell that the next year everyone would want a colored face mask, and they'd make a fortune. Sure enough, the next year all the companies found a way to make them, and every team wanted them.

3

GETTING IN THE GROOVE

Training Camp

For training camp in July of 1973, the Chargers moved the team to the University of California at Irvine, about seventy miles from San Diego. I'd been with the team since April and had practiced attaching facemasks until I could affix one in the dark. I knew that helmets—if they were to be safe—must fit exactly right. I had the locker room by the tail and could swing it in any direction. But moving the entire locker room—as I had to do for training camp—was an entirely different hurdle.

The moving company we used took two days to pack, transport, and unload 20,000 pounds of equipment for the equipment, training, weight, film, and front office departments. We moved enough supplies to last 45 days, including four secretary's desks, chairs, and typewriters. We even moved goal posts and goal post pads. Joe, my 13-year-old son (whom I hired as a ball boy), Bronco, and I went up two weeks before the team to get the camp ready. Setting up the locker room for 100 plus players took a full seven days. Rookie or not, here they come.

Ball Boys

Four days before the players arrived for training camp, I became headmaster for eight star-struck, hormone-engorged, naïve ball boys—13- to 16-year-old privileged kids I had never met and hadn't chosen. One 13-year-old climbed out of his parents' car with a backpack, tennis rackets, skis, a bicycle, and other items one might use for a vacation—plus his brother.

"I don't know where you think you are," I said to him, "but this is not Club Med. None of those things are allowed. You'll get up at 5:30 and have bed check at 10:30. Now, haul your butt out of here, load that stuff back in your parents' car, and say good bye to your brother."

I gathered them around me, made them stand at attention, and stated my rules: "You're to address Mr. Klein and all the coaches by their first names at all times. To you their first name is Mr. Don't Forget It. Call me Sergeant Brooks, I mean Sid." For a moment I slipped back into Air Force mode. "You're not to go to any player's room unless you have wakeup duty. No driving equipment carts without prior approval. No caps in the dining room. No visiting the cheerleader's camp next door. You're to be on time for work. If you're late, you will not be fined, since you won't make much money. If you're late, you will owe me double time working—two minutes late, four minutes of work. Understand?" Everyone nodded, and I heard a few snickers. I knew they thought I was joking. They didn't know I'd been through basic training in the Air Force and was willing to tie their little butts into knots.

In spite of the additional responsibility of managing them, ball boys proved an essential part of training camp and the season. There's no competition in the league without spies, and I needed able-bodied agents. After the first year, I chose those who were racially diverse and good students. Some turned out to be entrepreneurs as well. I knew I'd hired the right guys when I caught a few of them trying to sell ice cream bars from the cafeteria to the kids at the weight loss camp next door. They swore they were doing community service. I smiled. Kids always have a good reason for what they do.

Ready Or Not

The 1973 draftees and free agents reported in the brunt of a scorching July heat wave, a week before the veterans arrived. Players who had starred in college football and were high draft picks showed up confident and arrogant. Free agents appeared humble and hopeful, and the players who had been traded demonstrated a juxtaposition of anger and relief. I'm only guessing that the anger they showed on their faces was directed at their previous team's administration for letting them go, and the relief they displayed when they saw their names on a new locker was due to having found another place to play.

The week before the veterans arrived, the rookies did a lot of loud talking, "watch me" accolades, and laughing and joking about veterans not being all that tough. And then on July 15 the beef landed in the house. Cid Edwards, 250 pounds of muscle, came in first. One of the new draft picks asked me, "Is he a linebacker?"

"No," I said. "He's a fullback." The rookies' mouths clamped shut, and the bragging changed to silent awe. When Russ Washington came in you could hear a fly fart. Nicknamed "Mt. Washington," Russ stood 6 foot, 6 inches and weighed 289 pounds. He was an offensive wall all by himself, had a twinkle in his eyes, and smiled like a friendly teddy bear. In spite of his kind demeanor, his presence on the field was threatening. None of the new players said a word as the locker room filled with the likes of Ira Gordon (6 foot, 3 inches; 270 pounds), Kevin Hardy (6 foot, 5 inches; 276 pounds), Coy Bacon (6 foot, 4 inches; 270 pounds), and Doug Wilkerson (6 foot, 3 inches; 250 pounds with a 32-inch waist).

Deacon Jones—6 foot, 4 inches, 272 pounds, red-eyed, and snorting like he wanted to hit somebody—arrived in a loud, double-do talking, tambourine-shaking, awe-inspiring jubilee, as though leading a gospel revival. I forgot I was not there to watch the parade, and momentarily stared with my mouth wide open. These giants were joined by players with names that made sports headline news: Johnny Unitas, Mike Garrett, and Gary Garrison were only a few of them.

I received a lot of pats on the back, and maybe it was due to the players seeing someone like me in a position that was new to them. Al Cowlings, a young black player with the Buffalo Bills at the time, celebrated when he saw me, despite mistaking me for the janitor. Even the position of janitor was a novelty for a black man in an NFL locker room. When someone told him I was the equipment manager for the Chargers, he almost sent out a bulletin over the wire. He ventured into the hostile territory of the Chargers' locker room to congratulate me. But before long, everyone had settled into the business of preparing for the season, and I became just one of the men.

Duane Thomas and the Freaky Team Meeting

One super talent stands out as unforgettable in the memory of my honeymoon year with the Chargers. Remembered not only for his athleticism, Duane Thomas—a handsome, caramel-skin running back—appeared bizarre in that he isolated himself from everyone on the team and spoke to no one in the Chargers' camp except my son, Joe, and a couple of the other ball boys. Once in a while he'd utter to them a one-syllable sound, like a grunt from a vocabulary that had once contained words. Duane, a mixed-up young man, had been traded to the Chargers from Dallas that year. We'd heard about his talent, but he astonished the rest of us with behavior we considered strange. Duane didn't want to talk about it. He didn't want to talk, period.

Upon arriving in camp, Duane attended the team meeting dressed to the nines in a suit, while the other players wore workout clothes, shorts, T-shirts, and flip-flops. All of the players took seats in the meeting room, except for Duane. Harland

Svare, the head coach, asked Duane to be seated so he could start the meeting. Somber faces of the other team members hung toward their laps, waiting to see what Duane would do. No one dared look at him directly. Duane continued standing in the middle of the room, legs crossed at the ankles, a position he assumed most of the time, and stared blank-faced at Harland. He didn't answer, and he didn't sit down. Harland tried to catch Deacon's eye for a hint on how to handle the situation, but Deacon, usually in everybody's business, laid his head on his hands and offered not a peep. That was the first time I'd seen Deacon Jones have nothing to say.

Some people are more afraid of someone they *think* is crazy than someone they *know* is crazy. The players didn't know quite what to think about Duane, but many thought he was nuts. Harland went on with his meeting, glancing at Duane out of the corners of his eyes. Duane never moved. When the meeting ended, the other players and coaches got up from their seats and eased out of the meeting room around him. No one laughed. Harland and the players decided Duane could do whatever he wanted, because on the field talking was not required. And out there, Duane had what it took.

Sign Language at the Equipment Window

I was as busy as the flagman at the Daytona Speedway with the onset of two-a-day practices in training camp. On the second day of camp, just before the afternoon practice, I was in the equipment room swallowed in shoes when Duane Thomas came to the locker room, got dressed in most of his gear, and stood in front of me near the equipment window. We laid his gear out for him before he arrived at camp, so I thought maybe I'd forgotten something. The fact that Duane wouldn't talk had already been established, since he hadn't spoken to any of us. He didn't say anything this time, but stood in front of the window holding his jersey with the shoulder pads stuck inside. Some of the players placed their shoulder pads inside their jerseys, so they could slip them on as one unit. Duane stared at me, holding his jersey. I knew he wanted something, but I wasn't sure what.

"Can I help you, Duane?" I asked. He gave me a vacant look. I wasn't really afraid of him, but his silence was freakish. I shrunk back from the window, gathered my nerve, and asked again, "What can I do for you?"

He glanced down at his shoulder-padded jersey and then up at me again.

"You want me to do something for you, Duane? You need something?" I scanned the locker room for an interpreter, but there was no one around. Everyone except for the two of us had already gone to the practice field. He stared at me and made a scissor-like motion with his fingers. "You want me to cut something?" I asked. He mumbled, nodded slightly, made the motion again, and held out his jersey. I took a pair of scissors from my tool supply and cut off the bottom of his practice jersey. He slipped it over his head, put his helmet on, and left without a word.

I followed him out to the field to see what he'd do next. Coach Harland sent him in on a play a little while later and Duane ran the ball hard. The play called for Duane to catch the ball in midfield. He took off running in his high-top black shoes like a champion Greyhound. Johnny Unitas released the ball, and it sailed in the air far ahead of Duane. It appeared uncatchable. I heard coaches and players around me mutter the words "oh-no" and "damn." But on that day, we were all about to receive an eye-opener.

We knew that Duane could do his thing: run with the ball. But he could catch it, too, as we were about to find out. His feet barely brushed the ground as he raced down the field, his cut-off jersey flapping above his waist. Twisting his body and reaching out, he made a spectacular one-handed grab without ever looking up at the ball. He was every bit the player that had wowed fans, coaches, and fellow football players in Dallas. A chant went up amongst the players, "Duane is back ... Duane is back."

But to Duane the chants meant little. He headed back into his own little world without acknowledging his amazing feat or saying a word to anyone. Duane was all about football, and nothing else seemed to interest him.

Duane's Friends Or Not

Later that same afternoon, three young men strutted onto the practice field. The mid-afternoon heat in Irvine was unbearable; it may have been 100 degrees, but it felt five times as hot. Everyone on that field was drenched as if we'd survived a sudden downpour of rain. The three intruders, however, were laid-back, with an attitude and air about them as cool as a breeze off the ocean. They sported ankle-length, black leather coats, and walked out near mid-field. One of them shoved his hand into his coat pocket, at which point Deacon shouted, "They got guns."

Players, ball boys, and coaches ran for cover like dice rollers in a raided craps game. I didn't think Deacon could run as fast as he did, but he made it off the field and behind a barricade before anyone else. Some big guys hit the dirt, but like a good soldier on a battlefield, I stayed near Coach Harland's side. "Get them off the field," he said. I assumed he meant for me to get the crashers off the field; there was nobody else out there. So I approached the gunslingers as a band of helmets peeked over the top of the barricade like soldiers behind a fort wall. By this time, the trio had advanced to within a couple of feet of us, and the one guy still had his hand in his pockets.

Coach bristled. "What are you doing interrupting my practice? What do you want?"

"We're friends of Duane Thomas," one said. "We've come to try out for the team."

"Get the hell off my practice field," Harland said. They must have realized Harland didn't play, because they laughed it off and strolled back the way they'd come.

One by one the cowering soldiers crawled out from under cover, and Harland took one look at the distracted bunch and called off practice for the rest of the day. Meanwhile, Duane stood in the middle of the practice field with his helmet in his hands, as if he couldn't understand what was holding up practice. He never once glanced at the interruption or acknowledged the crashers. Of course, no one forgot what happened, and the incident soon became a running joke: "Who ducked for cover first?" We never discovered if the men were really friends of Duane's or not. Nor did we ever discover whether or not any of them were actually armed.

I saw Duane Thomas years after he left the Chargers, and we enjoyed a very genial conversation together—which is surprising considering how little he actually talked to me during that 1973 preseason camp. He had come a long way by that time from the troubled young man he was in the '70s. I'm happy to say he looked well, adjusted, and successful.

Stronger Than An Ox

A sled is a piece of heavy, padded, iron equipment used in practice to teach football players the proper way to block. Huge iron springs hold the sled together. The players practice blocking by slamming their bodies against the sleds in the same way they would attempt to tackle an opposing player. An unofficial NFL rule states that if a player breaks a sled with a hit during practice, he is automatically excused from practice for the rest of the day. Needless to say, that rule is hardly ever put to use, as it's rare for a player to prove his worth against an assembly of iron.

During practice one day Deacon went one-on-one with a sled and the sled fell apart. "Over here," Deacon yelled as soon as it happened. "Come see what I did to this sissy iron man." By that time in his career, Deacon wasn't all that strong, and the spring in the sled must have rusted and weakened, giving Deacon the advantage when he struck it.

Harland called the players together and said, "Deacon is finished for the day because he's broken a sled." Cheers and whistles went up. For ten minutes no one did anything except laugh, because, for ten minutes Deacon ranted, "Man you should have seen me slap that sucker and make it cry. I made it fall at my feet. That sucker went down and kissed the ground." He then took a victory lap around the field, waving his hands in the air, while the other players cheered him on.

Dave Costa and
Tim Rossovich—Tricksters

Dave Costa and Tim Rossovich were roommates at camp. While the rest of the team went about training camp with a serious attitude, those two were clowns. Every day, Costa was chauffeured the hundred or so yards from the dorms to the practice field by Rossovich in Costa's car—an aged black Cadillac sedan, long and gracious as a limousine, with deep black leather seats and a rattle that coughed like an old man with consumption. Their teammates said they were just plain wild and crazy. Now, when I look back on it, I think they did things to ease the pressure some guys were under about making the team. I don't think Costa and Rossovich cared if they made the team or not. Coming from the disciplined world of the military, I had never witnessed anyone like them, and the ball boys soon learned to avoid those two.

Ball boys had been instructed not to enter a player's room for any reason other than to wake a player who didn't answer to the knock of wakeup call. Ball boys were sent in pairs for wakeup duty. One morning the two ball boys knocked on Rossovich and Costa's door, and no one answered. They knocked again and still no answer. The ball boys looked at each other and grinned. "We're going in," one said, and the other nodded. This was their opportunity to get inside the player's room, and have something to brag to the other ball boys about.

From the doorway the room was dark, the curtains drawn. A still lump rested in the middle of each bed with the covers pulled up over the pillows. The ball boys heard snoring coming from both sides of the room and assumed Costa and Rossovich were still sleeping. So they entered the room and went to the beds to shake the sleeping players awake. Out of nowhere, Costa jumped down from the ceiling rafters onto one of the beds yelling like Tarzan, and Rossovich roared out of the closet on his motorcycle and popped a wheelie in the middle of the floor.

The boys scurried out into the hall—scared to death—and from that day on I couldn't get any of the ball boys to wake Costa and Rossovich for the remainder of camp. I had to do it myself. But Tim and Dave wouldn't dare pull that sort of a stunt on me, because I had what they needed when it came to equipment. They were actually protective of me. Every day Costa came by and checked on me. "You all right? Anybody giving you any grief? I don't want to have to kick nobody's ass this morning."

They were pranksters who had a good time and never harmed anyone, but the amazing part was that they never got punished for anything they did. The reason is simple: on Sunday, they played football.

Not a Rock Star

Tradition had it that all rookies must sing in training camp. Players, coaches, ball boys, equipment men, trainers—anyone new to the club—all fell into the rookie category. Singing took place when the team gathered in the camp dining room for dinner. Dinner began at 6:30, so I did my best to avoid the ritual. Slick as a con man, I went to dinner at 5:30 and left at 6:10 to get out of singing. I couldn't sing and didn't want to embarrass myself.

But the team wised up to me. One day I arrived at my usual time and the whole team was waiting for me. The three biggest men on the team—Lionel Aldridge, Russ Washington, and Doug Wilkerson—stood like sentries, arms folded across their chests, at the exits to the dining room. I crept to a table and sat down.

Carl Mauck stood up and pointed toward me. "Rookie, sing," he demanded. I continued to sit there for a minute try-

ing to think of a way to get out of singing. And then a chorus
of players yelled, "Get up and sing, Rookie." I struggled to my
feet, knocking over my chair as I stood up. Right up front, Joe
Beauchamp—"High Rev." we called him because his daddy was
a preacher—looked like the cat that had cornered a bird. Bobby
Howard—a fellow defensive back and Joe's partner in crime, so
to speak—stood next to Joe sporting a grin as wide as Mission
Valley.

"Come up front and stand on this chair and sing, Rookie,"
it seemed the whole team said. Someone yelled, "What's your
name and where did you come from? Sing your school song." I
dragged my feet up to the front of the dining room and sang in
Japanese the few words I'd learned while stationed in Japan in
the '50s, "Ohayo gozaimasu watakushi wa doko benjo." I didn't
translate for the players, but some of what I'd said was, "Good
morning. Where's the toilet? I need to take a dump." Everyone
cheered and clapped, none the wiser.

The next morning Joe stopped me in the locker room.
"You were going to sing one way or the other," he told me. I still
believe Joe—although I never got him to admit it—had watched
me and told the others about my early dinners. After my debut,
I went to dinner at 6:30 sharp and laughed, along with everyone
else, when the rest of the rookies were forced to sing. In all my
years with the team, I never heard a player who didn't think he
was a rock star during those singing situations. Some knew they
were headed for a recording studio, and others were so bad they
made dogs howl as far away as Santa Ana.

Acing the Real Test

On Saturday, August 4, 1973, the Chargers played the
New York Giants at San Diego. It was my first NFL game as
equipment manager. Every game during training camp was a
road trip, because even when we played at home we still had
to pack for the trip from Irvine to San Diego. During my years
with the Chargers, sports writers like Nick Canepa have commented on my preparedness, sometimes in jest. But still, I must

have checked the equipment ten times prior to my first game to make sure we'd packed every jersey. I asked the ball boys to check each bag the players had packed to take to San Diego to make sure each player's equipment was complete with numbers on the bags.

My stomach curled in knots when the bus turned into the stadium parking lot, and it stayed that way while the players dressed out. Like a first sergeant, I inspected each one as they left the locker room, to make sure they were wearing the correct socks, their jerseys were tucked in, and their helmets were shining.

That year, the Chargers had a contract to wear Adidas shoes. Johnny Unitas' black, high-top shoes—a trademark of his—weren't Adidas. So, we painted them blue with stripes designed to resemble those on Adidas shoes. I was only in Game One of my career as an equipment manager, but I had already learned that I had to do whatever was necessary in order to make the players feel comfortable.

When I emerged from the tunnel that day and caught sight of the fans in the stands, the goal posts standing ready, and the immensity of the playing field, larger and more grand than the makeshift practice fields we'd used for the past month, the knot in my stomach uncurled. I ran back up the ramp to the tunnel and threw up. One man from the maintenance crew saw me. "That must have been some bad food," he said and smiled knowingly. My stomach stayed queasy throughout the game and settled down only after the game ended.

The Chargers lost 28-3 and went 1-5 for the preseason. Our only win came against the Eagles, 24-17. In my naivete, I thought we were on our way to the Super Bowl.

4

INSIDE THE CHARGERS' LOCKER ROOM

A Peek Inside for a Future Charger

One day in the mid-'80s, I was at my desk in my office checking receipts when I looked up and saw a high school kid sneak into the locker room. Tanned and muscular, he looked as if he belonged in a pro uniform already. Two high school teams were scheduled to play a championship game in the stadium that afternoon. Anyone could follow the tunnel from the field and end up in the locker room. It was during the off-season, so the locker room was empty of players, and the lockers were empty except for helmets.

I kept quiet, watching him peering about the place until he saw me and hesitated.

"What do you want?" I asked.

"I just want to touch Dan Fouts' helmet, sir," he said, "before you throw me out."

"Go ahead," I said. "But then you'll have to leave."

I smiled, knowing I would never throw a kid out of the locker room. Dan kept a soft chair in front of his locker. The kid went straight to Dan's locker, took down his helmet and rubbed it.

"Here, you can sit on his chair too if you want to," I said, awed by his admiration for the quarterback.

He sat down with the helmet in his hands as though he were carrying the king's crown. He never said a word, but his eyes glowed, and he smiled as winsome as the Mona Lisa. After sitting for a while and stroking the helmet, he took it back to Dan's locker, said, "Thank you, Sir," and left.

A few minutes later, I looked up, and he had come back with six or eight other kids. I heard him tell them, "Come on. It's okay; I know this man. He's my friend." I had to laugh at the audacity of the kid, but I let them in. They stayed a short while, holding Dan's helmet and smiling. They were about to leave, and I said to the one who'd claimed to be my friend, "Hey, kid, what's your name?"

He looked at me, showed all his teeth in a big smile, and answered, "Junior Seau."

Mr. Brooks, if You Please

I had been the Chargers equipment manager for ten years when Bob Wick became my assistant at the end of the 1982 season. Bronco left to head the equipment department for the San Francisco 49ers, and Bob filled his spot. Even though he was just a baby-faced 23-year-old, Bob had been a ball boy and he knew his way around the locker room. It was hardly likely that he'd be mistaken for the department head. Salesmen called and made appointments to show me the new line from sporting goods companies. I knew most of the top brass of quite a few sporting goods companies from my years at the Air Force Academy, but none of the salesmen were aware of that in the beginning. Every one of those salesmen, on their first visit, walked past me and addressed Bob as "Mr. Brooks," even when I was sitting behind my desk in my office.

"I'm not Mr. Brooks," Bob would say, pointing to me. "That's the man you want to see." After a while Bob and I had a little routine going. We'd go through the "I'm not Mr. Brooks" thing, and then I'd excuse myself and leave the salesman sitting in my office, promising I'd come right back. Not a single one of them ever apologized for the mistake of assuming that Bob was the man in charge and not I. That was a mistake in itself.

I would leave the salesman sitting in my office long enough to begin to wonder, "Who the hell is this guy?" My office was decorated with my Air Force accomplishments, photos of me receiving awards from generals, and autographed photos of United States presidents. My office was decorated in a way that would lead others to believe that I had met and was friendly with most of the world. I wanted those salesmen to believe that. It was better than saying, "You'll remember me next time."

When I would return, the salesman would often whirl around and say, "You know a lot of people, don't you?"

"Let's just get to business and talk about the jerseys you came to show me," I would reply. I soon earned a reputation around the league as someone who should be dealt with fairly and squarely. To respectfully borrow and paraphrase a passage from Sidney Poitier's book *The Measure of a Man*: "My work was me, and I tried my damnedest to take good care of me, because I was taking care of the me that represented a hell of a lot more than me." I was taking care of all the dark-skinned men who would come after me.

The Green Book

The locker room crew hung the coaches' shirts, pants, and jackets on a bar in their lockers, three fingers apart. The belt hung on a hook on the right side, caps on the left side of the shelf facing out. Underwear was placed on the right of the seat, game program on the left, shoes on the floor on the left, new socks on top of shoes, and a stool placed on the right. Each locker was prepared in the exact same way. A hotline existed between the NFL equipment men, nicknamed "The Green Book."

Because I wanted every new coach who came to work with us to feel special, as soon as I heard that one had been hired, I called the equipment manager of the team that coach had been with and gathered information that went into the green book. My book contained everything from the coach's clothing size to the type of sled he preferred to use in practice. When a new coach walked into the locker room, his name was on his locker, and he didn't have to ask for anything: it was all there waiting for him. I always got the same astonished question, "How did you know all this?" And each time I answered, "That information is top secret."

Tricks of the Trade

During the week, I played tricks in the locker room and teased the players, but on game day I put on a different face. I took the game seriously, and respected the players' need for a place to prepare for the contest. I might have stretched the rules a bit when it came to getting my team ready for the game, but not enough to get caught. I did not do anything that I now regret.

Before all games, at home and on the road, all the offensive linemen went out for pregame warmup, came back in the locker room before the game, went into the shower, and stood in a circle with a towel over their heads. No one said anything; they just waited for me to come in. I sprayed their jerseys with Silicone spray. I rubbed it in and made sure it was distributed under the sleeves as well. Silicone made the jerseys slick, which made it difficult for the opposing team to grab the jerseys. Remembering my own spies back home, on the road I scouted out the facility, making sure we'd have a secret room away from the eyes of the visiting locker room attendant for our jersey prep.

Sand Knit made our jerseys. I asked them to make us a jersey with a shiny material so the referees couldn't tell that anything had been applied to the jersey. That didn't stop opposing players from complaining, however. Prepared as always for an interrogation, I pulled a new shirt out of the bag and showed the referee the shiny new material. As they say—all's fair in love and war.

A New Owner

In 1984 when Mr. A.G. Spanos became owner of the San Diego Chargers, I had grown comfortable in my niche in the locker room. It was designed, rearranged, organized, and kept up with minimal fault in a manner that reflected my professionalism. I had Bob, an assistant whom I could depend on. He knew how I wanted the locker room maintained. We were both proud that at any time of day our locker room was presentable.

Three months after Mr. Spanos acquired ownership of the Chargers, the upstairs offices had been ripped apart and had taken on a much-needed fresh look that reflected the new owner's style. We could see things would be different cosmetically, and that was a good thing. These offices lined a hallway that led to the owner's big office. The walls along the hallway were knocked down and replaced with oak posts supporting large glass panels from floor to ceiling. When Mr. Spanos walked down the hall it was possible to see everyone at work at their desk. Every Tuesday, Mr. Spanos flew in on his private jet. When his plane landed, a call came into the switchboard, "The Eagle has landed." The source of this information has never been revealed. I wouldn't give it away if I knew. Some things are better kept under wraps. Ten minutes later an announcement came over the intercom, "The Eagle is approaching; man your desks."

Mr. Spanos always wore a sweater tied across his shoulders in a classy-style. He was impeccably dressed, a reflection of the way in which he surrounded himself with class. When he walked down the hall to his office, everyone appeared to be working very hard, their faces intent on the job at hand, while a sly look passed between them, apprehensive I guess, as all employees are of a new boss. He didn't stop to greet any of them. To him, the really important stuff waited behind the doors in the big office.

I knew sooner or later he'd come down and put his seal on the locker room. I was ready, although I had not faced an inspection from anyone in the organization before. In the past, the locker room had not been high on the priority list for achieving a winning football team. Bob fiddled around, ran into things, and jumped at the sound of the walls creaking in anticipation of the boss's arrival, but being an old military man, an inspection was just a stroll in Balboa Park for me. I'd been on the Inspector General's team in my previous job. One day after The Eagle had landed, I'd gone up to meet with the coaches, when Bob called upstairs for me.

"Mr. Spanos is down here," he said, "and he wants to see you."

"What does he want to see me about?" I asked.

"I don't know," Bob said. "But he's waiting for you, now."

"Where is he?"

"He's at the front door of the locker room," Bob replied.

"Tell him I'll be right down." I took the elevator down to the back door and entered the locker room from the rear, near the training room. I could see Mr. Spanos standing with his back to me, near the front door with some of his executives and friends. I made very quiet steps across the locker room, and didn't speak until I was close enough to breathe down his neck. At that point, I said very loudly, "Mr. Spanos, did you want to see me?"

He jerked around. I knew he'd expected me to come through the front door, and he hesitated as though he had forgotten why he'd asked for me. "I want you to keep this locker room clean at all times," he said, and looked around. "The way it is now."

The locker room was shipshape beyond criticism. I smiled and said, "Yes, Sir." Bob sneaked off to the office out of sight. I kept my lips peeled back in a smile. "And I want you to make sure the helmets are shined at all times," he continued. I gathered he was trying to wipe the smile off my face and reaching for something to help shape me up, but I'd made sure there was little to improve.

"Excuse me, Mr. Spanos," I said. "We might have a problem with some of the players about their helmets. Doug Wilkerson and Charlie Joiner do not want their helmets polished." I had learned to respect idiosyncrasies and superstitions of players on game day. They trusted me, because I had never before intentionally disappointed one of them. It was their comfort and confidence that helped improve their game. I had seen that. No matter how shined the helmets were, five minutes after a game started, the helmets would be smeared with mud, blood, and grass-stains. But the equipment department always sent them out shining like new.

"I want all the helmets shining," he retorted.

"Yes, Sir," was all I said. That was Tuesday, the players' day off. The following day I told Doug and Charlie that the owner wanted their helmets polished and shining.

"Do what you have to do, Doc," Charlie said. "And you know I'll do what I have to do." Charlie wouldn't wear anything that looked new. So I couldn't wait to see what he would do.

Bob and I, along with one of our part-time assistants, spent 20 man-hours polishing all of the helmets. On Sunday before the game, Charlie Joiner took his shining helmet to the bathroom and banged it against the walls until it was roughed up and looked thoroughly used. Charlie said, "He said you had to shine it; he didn't say I had to wear it shining."

"Don't worry about it, Doc," Doug said. "I can still play."

That week we played a night game in Seattle. Of course, under the lights of the dome, the helmets glittered and gleamed as though they had two halos—even Charlie's.

Kangaroo Court

Players were brought up on charges in "kangaroo court" during training camp for any number of reasons, and usually by an anonymous accuser. The so-called criminals knew something would happen to them if they didn't carry out their sentence.

Sitting behind a desk with the accused to his left, James "Shack" Harris was juror and judge. Any player brought to court

was guilty until proven guilty. There was no such thing as inno-
cence. The accused was required to dress in a suit, shirt, and tie.
Shorts, T-shirts, or any Chargers' gear was unacceptable. The
accused was allowed to bring a "lawyer"—essentially a teammate who happened to play the same position—but it was only
for show as the lawyer was not permitted to speak. A crowd of
teammates gathered in the courtroom, which was the vestibule
between the dorm rooms. There'd be a lot of "Tsk, tsking," and
"Ah, that's not fair" from the spectators.

The charges were often ridiculous in nature. Lionel
James—who stood just 5 feet, 9 inches—was brought before
Judge Shack. "Charges have been brought against you," Harris
stated, "for being too short to see over the dashboard of your car.
What do you have to say in your defense?"

Lionel opened his mouth to speak, but Shack cut him off,
"Guilty as charged," he said. Lionel hung his head, as laugh-
ter exploded around him. Someone said, "Cut him some slack,
Shack." Another countered, "Give him the max."

Shack handed out the punishment: "You are hereby sen-
tenced from now on to increase your vision from the car by
placing two telephone books under your butt on the driver's seat
of your car to raise yourself up."

Larue Harrington was another player brought before the
judge. I'm not saying how the judge got wind of his crime, but
Larue had been caught red-handed. We ordered gray under-
shorts for the players to wear under their football pants. We
knew we were losing quite a few to theft, suspecting that the
players had taken them home. We marked "Third Team" on
the back of the shorts, smack over the butt. That didn't stop the
shorts from disappearing, however, so we cut a big round hole
out of the shorts over the wedge of the butts, smack-dab over the
butt crack. One of our people saw Larue in a shopping center
wearing a pair of shorts with his butt showing through the hole.

"What do you have to say in your defense?" Shack asked.

"Not..." is as far as Larue got.

"Guilty as charged," Shack said. "You are hereby confined
to camp for seven days, and you must count all the shorts with
holes cut out of the butt every day."

We brought charges against players for all sorts of things, sometimes just to have some fun at the rookies' expense. No one ever checked to see if the sentences were carried out, but rookies were too afraid not to follow through with the sentencing.

A New Look

Mr. Spanos called me upstairs for a meeting with him, Steve Ortmeyer (director of football operations), and Rick Smith (head of public relations).

"I want to change the uniform," he said. "I want you to take that lightning bolt off and make a uniform that looks something like Miami's."

"Yes, Sir," I said. This was the second time in my Charger career that I'd been asked to design a new look for the Chargers.

"Get some samples made up without the bolts," continued Spanos. "Let's see what you come up with."

I had some samples made up, but I didn't like any of them, so I never showed him any of them. On the way back from a game in Texas, we flew through a rainstorm. I looked out of the plane's window and the lightning flashed white against the dark blue sky. "Bob," I said to my assistant. "I've got it."

"What?" he wondered.

"I've got the new design for the uniform. See the white lightning?"

Bob looked out at the lightning and agreed with my concept. I had a uniform made up with the white bolts on the sides of the pants, on the jersey, and on the helmet, and Bob modeled it for Mr. Spanos.

"That's it," he said. "That's the one I want."

The Chargers used "Design by Sid Brooks" for many years thereafter.

Bragging Will Make You Humble, Or Worse

A majority of the players minded the rules of the locker room, but there was always someone who brought disorder to our carefully organized insanity. Each year a new player with an ego bigger than his talent descended upon us. Bronco and I had overheard plenty of the egotistical chattering of men headed out the door before they'd barely been welcomed inside.

In preseason, we would assign two or three rookies to one locker. The veterans and returning players each had a locker to themselves. By the time the roster had been settled, the lockers would be down to one player per. Martin French, a free agent wide receiver, came in spouting his knowledge before he received his gear. He was full of himself and talking as if time was running out (which, in his case, it was). He claimed he was every bit as good a receiver as the all-pro Charlie Joiner. He told us he should have a locker on the side with the veterans because he was the best receiver in the NFL, the all-time best.

Bronco and I looked at each other. "Okay," I thought to myself, "if you're so smart, we'll give you a lesson you won't forget." I decided to introduce him to the big boys, and I gave him his own locker between Charlie Joiner and Dan Fouts. Then I told the veterans why we had put him there. I didn't have to say anything else, knowing the veterans would teach him a thing or two on their own.

One other rookie asked Martin, "How do you rate a locker with the vets?"

Martin's response: "Because I told the people in the equipment room that I know I'll make the team."

In the ensuing days following practice, the veterans threw their dirty clothes in Mr. Super Star's locker. Every day he had to clean it all out and put each players clothing in the appropriate locker. One day the vets took things a step further, throwing not only their dirty clothes into his locker, but also their helmets, pads, and shoes. By this time he'd lost his desire to brag, but he stayed put and cleaned up after the veterans every day.

We issued socks and jocks to all players without question, and we weren't behind the treatment he received from the veterans, but Martin felt so intimidated after a while that he asked Charlie Joiner to get socks for him from the equipment guys. Charlie was always compassionate, and he wasn't afraid of losing his job to a big mouth, so he'd go to the equipment window and get socks for Martin. This went on for three days before we caught on. We realized Charlie was using a lot of socks, and we watched him to see what he was doing with them. The next day, we cut half the foot off the socks and folded them over before we handed them to Charlie, and then we all watched while Martin pulled the halved socks over his feet. We would have given him the socks, if he'd asked.

Martin's most humbling day came when Jimmy Hammond, the trainer, went around the locker room and gathered up all the dirty clothes from the whole team and taped them in place in Martin's locker with adhesive tape. "Be careful what you ask for," he wrote across the tape. Getting cut before the season started proved Martin French's saving grace. We missed him.

The Gold Card

I catered to the players. I spoiled them so much that I received calls from those that had been traded to other teams asking me to send them shoes or some little item that I had invented to add comfort to their gear. Before the salary cap and the collective bargaining agreement, coaches handed out gifts after a win to players who had performed outstandingly in the game. These gifts would be anything from cash or watches, to radios and TVs. Keoki Kamau, our head trainer at the time, saw an American Express ad flashing a gold card on TV one night and thought, "Hmm. We can do that." The next morning he presented the idea to the dungeon rats. "How about if we pick our own outstanding player of the game each week and present him with our Gold Card Award?"

We all agreed. The recipient of our award was not the outstanding player of the week chosen by the press, but an unsung hero, the guy in front of the big-name stars who made the plays that helped the stars shine. It was our way of giving a player recognition that he would not have otherwise received.

I ordered special jackets, caps, and T-shirts with Gold Card Winner on them. After the game, the Gold Card committee, made up of the locker room staff, picked the winner and put his name on the jacket. When the players arrived on Wednesday, we announced that week's winner.

The Gold Card granted priority in the locker room and training room. If I was fitting a player out, and the Gold Card winner wanted something, the player I'd been helping had to wait while I stopped to assist the winner. If a player was on the training table getting taped, and the Gold Card winner wanted to get taped, the player on the table had to get off to make room for the winner. Anything the winner wanted—even a massage— was his.

Our Gold Card winner was served donuts and orange juice Wednesday through Friday. Every morning, he received two newspapers—the *San Diego Union* and *USA Today*—in his locker. If the game that week happened to be a playoff game, our Gold Card winner was served a full breakfast on Friday, cooked in the trainer's room so the rest of the team could smell it. The winner often asked us to wait for a full house before we cooked the bacon. The aroma would drift through the locker room, and then we would serve him in front of his teammates.

On Friday, a limo picked the winner up at his house and drove him to work. After practice, the same limo would take him home. And that was the end of his Gold Card privileges for the week. The next morning he caught hell from the players he had harassed.

The award drew all kinds of attention from the team. Guys began predicting that they'd be the next winner. "Watch me. I'm going to get that Gold Card," we heard them say. They had no idea how we picked a winner—but did they ever want to win. Things progressed to the point where nothing mattered to the players as much as getting the card—not player of the game or the game ball. Nothing topped the Gold Card.

We didn't know what we were in for when we presented the card to rookie running back Eric Bieniemy. At 5 feet, 7 inches, he strutted around the locker room like a peacock. He sat and waited for a veteran player to get on the training table and to be taped up before he asked him to get off. He was a little Julius Caesar among the big men.

But the idea was a brilliant one, even if it sometimes pitted rookies against vets. The dungeon rats believed that with our little gift we had contributed to the intensity of the play on the field. We understood that the incentive for excellent football has been, and always will be, winning.

Gift Giving—A Part of the Game

Each week for a couple of years in the '90s, I gave the coaching staff and players a small token for winning games. I called the president of Starter Clothing Company on Monday and asked him to donate promotional items for every man in the football department. He sent light jackets, vests, caps, sweaters, stocking caps, or shirts so that they arrived on Wednesday. I placed one of the gifts in each man's locker on Thursday after practice.

The players took care of me in return; although I would have done my best to make every aspect of their locker room experience a good one regardless. They were very generous toward me, and each year they showed their appreciation to me in different ways. Courtney Hall, Broderick Thompson, and Harry Swayne saw to it that I was dressed in tailor-made suits, a new one each year. As long as my son, Michael, and his friend, Rocky Baham—both of whom were equipment assistants for the team—kept their grades up, Carlos Bradley and Kellen Winslow rewarded them every week with spending money. Lydell Mitchell even gave my son his first car, then bought it back from him only to turn around and give it right back to my son—free of charge. Each year in the league, my football family grew and grew.

Tough Guy

One might think that most football players are tough, fearless warriors who laugh in the face of danger, whether real or imagined. That is far from the truth. In fact, in some respects, they are just as frail as the everyday man on the street.

Wide receiver Shawn Jefferson wasn't a large guy. He stood just 5 feet, 11 inches, and carried maybe 185 pounds on his frame. But after hearing him talk, you'd swear that he was John Henry, Paul Bunyan, and Samson all rolled into one. For a little guy he talked big and was not shy about it. But more impressively, he played up to his self-proclaimed "greatness" on the field. He let it be known across the NFL that any defensive back who dared to play him in bump-and-run coverage was going to get embarrassed—and he backed that up when the time came.

This was Shawn for the entire world to see and marvel at. But down in the locker room he was appreciative of the "dungeon rats." Every practice day he came in with fresh specialty coffee for each of us, remembering just how each of us liked our coffee. On his last day with the team, he presented us with a feast fit for a king. It was this sort of thoughtfulness that characterized Shawn off the field and shows that players' off-field personalities sometimes differ considerably from their on-field demeanor. I can only tell the following tale because of Shawn's strength on the football field. His weakness in this instance makes him not a coward, but human, as we all are.

The Chargers had just come off two bruising games, and while victorious, some key players sustained a few injuries that needed immediate attention, including Shawn and 275-pound center Courtney Hall. Courtney was in the team doctor's office having his knee drained to treat his injury. The process of draining one's knee is not for anyone with an aversion to blood or long needles. In fact, even those who have been through this ritual without pause will tell you that it's difficult to not cringe during this process.

The doctor begins the procedure by cleaning the area that needs drained with an antiseptic agent. He then fills a small syringe with a local anesthetic and injects it into the area to be drained. This is done to prepare the area for the "real" needle—a 14-gauge, which tends to be four to five inches in length. Why so long? Well, most times, this needle has to penetrate layers of muscle and fat in order to get to the spot where the fluid has settled. It's enough to give the toughest of guys the heebie-jeebies.

Courtney was sitting on the examination table after the completion of his procedure by the team doctor when the doctor asked, "Courtney, do you mind talking with Shawn while we drain his knee?" Courtney thought that was a strange request. He had been in the doctor's office many times and this was the first time he had been asked to entertain another patient during a procedure, but he said, "Sure, Doc. I want to catch up with Shawn anyway." Courtney was about to see a whole different side of tough-man Shawn, the kind of stuff that went straight back into the locker room to be used for some wholesome teasing.

In the examining room, Courtney began chatting with Shawn while the doctor prepared his concoction. The doctor dipped a sponge in some antiseptic solution and began cleaning the area, and then a strange thing happened. Shawn stopped talking and began instead paying close attention to the procedure. The strange part wasn't that Shawn paid attention to the procedure (pro athletes generally want to know what is being done to their body), but that he stopped talking. Shawn had *never* been at a loss for words.

While the physician worked, the room went silent. He first filled the "small" needle, and Shawn began speaking very slowly but firmly, "Doc, make sure you don't hit my bone with that needle." Now, the team doctor had been doing this for quite a while. "I am positive that no bones will be touched by the needle," he assured Shawn. However, Shawn continued to direct him, "Keep away from my bone."

It was at that moment that Courtney understood why he had been asked to come in and sit with Shawn. As soon as Shawn was injected with the anesthesia he began to scream, "Doc you're on my bone! Arghhhhh!" Doc looked at Courtney and smiled. "I'm not anywhere near your bone," he told Shawn. Shawn screamed with a loud agonizing moan, "Yesssss you are. Arghhh!"

The first injection was over as soon as it began. Giving the anesthetic time to take affect, the doctor asked Shawn, "Are you sure you're ready for this?" "Yeah ... go ahead," Shawn responded in an aggrieved whisper. Before plunging the needle through the layers of Shawn's tissue, the doctor sprayed a stream of liquid nitrogen onto an area of his skin away from the actual injection area. As soon as the stream hit Shawn's skin, he began shrieking, "Doc! You're on my bone! You're on my bone!" Doc just chuckled, telling Shawn that he hadn't even done anything yet.

Courtney was astounded at Shawn's display of panic, but at the same time clenched his jaws shut to control his own laughter. Would anyone believe what he had witnessed? Doc finally gave Shawn's knee a jab through the muscle with the big, long needle. Shawn's facial expressions contorted into a pained look, and he let out another scream. "Arrrrrrghhhhhh! Doc, wait, wait, wait! You're on my bone! Stoooooooop!"

To fully drain Shawn's knee took approximately four minutes. During the procedure you can imagine what came out of his mouth—not his knee. When it was finished Shawn sat up and began talking again, as though Courtney and he had just struck up a conversation and the entire process had never happened, "Man, I'm going to kill the Broncos this week!" Shawn said. "They can't stop me! I'll be snatching balls out of the air right in front of them before they figure out which way I went. You know, C. Hall? They can't stop me!"

Yeah right. Off the doctor's table, Shawn was The Man. On it, not so much.

What Goes Up Must Come Down

Before relaying this story to you, there are some general facts that you should know, mainly because Courtney Hall would like me to stress that he is no different than most people. First, plenty of people dread being stuck on an elevator—claustrophobia is very common. Second, in stressful and presumably life-threatening situations, panic is a completely normal reaction. Finally, large people require more oxygen and therefore are more concerned about the relay time of elevator repair response teams, or as Courtney likes to call them, life-savers.

Today, the Chargers' in-season practice facility is a state-of-the-art facility located just miles from Jack Murphy Stadium.

This was not always the case, though. In fact, when Courtney played for the team over a decade ago, the offices and meeting rooms were on the second floor in Jack Murphy, and the practice field was a stone's throw away. Our lockers were in the basement, so most players caught elevators to get to meetings and to the practice field. But not *all* players.

Courtney claimed that due to a few tragic childhood events—which he states his psychiatrist said he's made progress getting over—elevators have been one of his least favorite modes of transportation. Actually, he was one of a handful of players who chose to bypass the elevators at the stadium and find alternate ways to get to meetings and to the practice field. Climbing stairs only added a few minutes to their commute, and the big guys could always use the exercise.

Well, Courtney was running late to a meeting one day, and stood to pay a hefty fine if he was late—$1,000 per minute. So he had no choice but to ride the elevator. Mind you, these elevators were very old and had a tendency to break down. He wonders to this day whatever possessed him to get on the elevator that day.

A bunch of players piled into the elevator, surpassing the maximum load by close to 800 pounds—three of them alone might have caused that to happen. That was the first bad sign. Then another player commented, "Courtney, I've never seen you on the elevator before. What gives?" That was the second sign. And to top it off, another heavy shoved his way onto to the elevator and blurted out, "I can't be late today! I've already lost $3,000 today for being late to my position meeting. I'm not going to be late again!"

The door closed and the elevator dropped a few inches. Everyone yelled a collective "Whoa." Courtney looked like he was thinking, "Oh crap," and turned a little green around his mouth. The elevator began its ascent with a groan, only to come to a protesting, sudden halt. Most of the players joked, "Great, we're going to be late!" Others kidded, "I guess I shouldn't have had that last biscuit for breakfast."

But Courtney was in no kidding mood. Perspiration gathered around the edges of his hairline as he began to hyperventilate. "What are we gonna do?" he gasped, as though the air had already closed in around him. "Does the phone work? Someone call. What about the emergency button? Press it." From the back of the elevator Courtney commanded a slew of solutions without making any effort to try any of them himself.

"Calm down, dude," someone said. "The elevator usually starts up after a few minutes. Calm down." Courtney had zoomed past the point of being consoled and was firmly into panic mode! With little room to move, he began squirming in his corner of the elevator. "I can't take it," he said. "Where's the ventilation? We aren't getting enough oxygen. We need help." The players muddled around for five minutes or so in the tight quarters of the elevator, and gave up on trying to keep Courtney calm. He curled up in a corner—resigned to his fate of being shot down in his prime—and tried to make himself take up as little space as possible, which was a losing feat.

Then someone said, "Man, we can't wait for the repair people to come. We're late. We're losing money." One of the offensive linemen pulled apart the elevator doors. To everyone's surprise, they saw open sky! The elevator, which opened to the outside of the building, had only missed the next floor by six inches or so. Everyone stepped out—except for Courtney, who made a mad dash—and hustled to the meeting.

Courtney was teased shamelessly for the next week or so.

Multiple Personalities

The late Derrick Thomas, a linebacker for the Kansas City Chiefs, was one of the premier pass rushers in the NFL. I believe his record of seven quarterback sacks in one game still holds. It was the Chargers' misfortune to face him a minimum of two times each year—three times if both teams made the playoffs.

During those years, we had a left tackle worthy of honorable mention, Harry Swayne. Although he never made the Pro Bowl, he was well respected throughout the NFL. In fact, the Chargers had so much confidence in his abilities, they routinely left him on an "island" to block a defender without any other help. He was up to the task most of the time. A competitor with soul, Harry often stayed late studying film of opponents, and he took pride in his footwork. But his specialty was pass blocking.

Early in the season, Harry was given the monumental task of shutting down Derrick Thomas. The scheme was for him to block Derrick all by himself so that the offense could change up and get more players into the pass pattern. On this occasion, Harry did a fabulous job against Derrick, allowing the extraordinary linebacker zero sacks and no pressures. The Chargers won the first game they played with the new scheme, and Harry was our "Player of the Week."

Since San Diego had prevailed with that blocking scheme earlier in the season, the Chargers didn't want to tinker around with success the next time they played the Chiefs. They employed the same plan for our second matchup. Harry was ready. Unfortunately, so was Derrick. I suppose that the thrashing Derrick had taken really lit a fire under him. He came out of the tunnel like a madman and racked up five sacks in the game. It was not a good day for Harry.

On Monday, which is usually the day the team reviews the game film, the offensive line met to critique their performance. Besides being extremely competitive, Harry was prone to wild mood swings. From one minute to the next, his personality might change from "All-American Boy" to something resembling the disposition of Brutus from the *Popeye* comics. Courtney Hall was directed by our coaching staff to monitor and regulate—as best he could—Harry's mood in that meeting, so that the offensive line could function cohesively. In other words, Courtney had to keep Harry from getting into fights with his teammates.

After his recent performance against Derrick Thomas, everyone knew that Harry was not going to be happy reliving it during their Monday film session. Our offensive line coach, Carl Mauck, slid the tape into the machine and began, "Men, we all are going to have rough days, but the key is how we recover. Let's get going." When the tape made it to the first sack Harry gave up, Coach responded, "Harry, you just took a bad set here.

See your first step? You've got to make sure that you step back, not up or sideways. Derrick is too fast; he'll beat you every time if you do that." Harry just grunted in response: "Yeah, I know."

After reviewing sack number two, Coach said: "Harry, Derrick just gave you an outside fake and came underneath. Your feet got crossed up a bit. Not a big deal." Harry remained silent this time. After reviewing the third sack, Coach said, "I think you know what happened here, Harry. Derrick just ..." At that instant, Harry leaped from his chair, tossed it against the wall, opened the door, and stormed down the hall. All the while, Coach screamed after him, "Harry! Harry!" But Harry didn't look back.

After the film, the team dressed for Monday practice. Harry was nowhere to be found. The head coach and offensive line coach asked after Harry's whereabouts, but no one knew where he was. During practice the rest of the offensive line took turns at Harry's position. The one great thing about offensive linemen or defensive linemen is that they form a brotherhood. The players always look out for one another. Unable to find Harry, the linemen practiced and went home. Wednesday, Harry appeared before his teammates and apologized. He knew that his teammates had had to take extra repetitions during practice, and he felt bad.

From that day forward, Harry Swayne was known as "Sybil," a man of many personalities.

5

ON THE ROAD

A Lesson in Blocking

The Chargers played the Redskins in Washington D.C. for my first regular-season road trip, and I was as shaky as a man facing his executioner. I arrived at the stadium six hours before the rest of the team; I was nervous and wanted to make sure that everything was in order.

The Chargers won the coin toss that day. With the kickoff the ball went into the end zone, and the game got underway on the 20-yard line. Mike Garrett lined up behind the quarterback, took the hand off from Johnny Unitas, and ran to the left. Mike was like a bullet shot from a gun in the open field, so linemen from opposing teams tried to pin him in quickly. On this carry, Mike got smacked hard for a loss. Two plays later, the quarterback handed the ball off to Mike again, and the defense swarmed him and down he went again. Walt Sweeney was the guard blocking for Mike. He was a seasoned veteran who knew his position, but that day it was clear that Walt was not at the top of his game. When one player does not carry through on his assignment, the system fails.

The offense came off the field, and Walt sat on the bench in front of me. Mike swaggered up to him snorting, heat radiating from him like a wild boar. Mike growled and complained about Walt's inability to block for him. Walt leaned back on the seat and let Mike rant and rave but didn't say anything in response. Back on the field, Mike got the call for the same play again, and immediately a Redskins' defense slammed into him and pushed him down onto the turf like an ambushed ant on his way to a food fest.

Walt, a devil-may-care Irishman with an attitude of his own, swaggered back to the huddle, bent over, and whispered in Mike's ear, "That's what happens when I don't block."

To Dress Or Not to Dress

In the early '70s, football players attended college in the age of self-expression and anti-establishment. Their rebellious nature included a lack of concern for proper wardrobe while on the road; players showed their disrespect by donning shorts, ripped pants with no underwear, and T-shirts with all sorts of logos on them. Before an upcoming road trip to Cleveland, head coach Harland Svare called a team meeting and addressed his players: "You must show respect for your family and your team. From now on, we will have discipline in our dress and appearance when we travel as a team. For all away games everyone will wear shoes, a whole pair of pants, jacket, and tie."

On Saturday before we left San Diego, some players drove their cars to the airport. At the gate everyone watched to see how other players had dressed. Some, mostly offensive linemen and defensive linemen, dressed in pink, powder-blue, purple, and lime-green leisure suits. The big guys were comfortable. Ten minutes before boarding time, Tim Rossovich had still not appeared. The minutes ticked by, and Coach kept checking his watch as the pilots had a scheduled take off. Just as everyone was ready to get on the plane, Tim strolled up wearing shoes, pants, a very nice silk tie, and a jacket—*covering his bare chest*. Harland marched up to him like a man on a mission. "I told you we will have discipline on this team and to come in proper attire."

Tim—his hair big, long, and curly, fanning out around his face—checked out his clothes, and then he glared up at Harland with eyes bright and wild as an untamed buck. "You didn't say anything about a shirt," he retorted.

Harland turned and shook his head. "Just get your ass on the plane," he said. Some of the guys laughed so loud, and I couldn't help but join in. Still, I made sure that coach didn't see me laughing. Tim was simply too much of a maverick to change.

A Secret Exit

A hostile atmosphere hung over San Diego Stadium following the Chargers' 19-0 loss to Kansas City on November 4, 1973, which marked the sixth game in a row the Chargers had failed to win. Their record stood at 1-6-1. Another loss for the Chargers prompted fans in the stands to hurl their dissatisfaction in the form of insulting comments, trash, beer cans, and coolers in the direction of the head coach as he tried to leave the field. Harland found himself deserted on the field, forced to escape alone. No one would walk beside him, as if he had the plague. His name was shouted—in non-endearing tones—from the stands, and the players—many of whom rushed into the tunnel that led to the locker room—left a wide space between themselves and Harland. Harland made it safely inside the locker room—but he still had to make it home.

Hecklers had surrounded the players' parking lot, waiting for the coach to get in his car to leave the stadium. The stadium manager popped his head out to check out the scene, and found that fans had surrounded the tunnel that led to the parking lot, and were chanting, "We want Harland. We want Harland."

The stadium manager headed to the locker room and told Harland, "You'd better not go out there. We'll have to get you out without them seeing you." The manager had the stadium crew load Harland's car—a brown Datsun 280-Z—onto a forklift and passed it through a large opening in the stadium wall onto the playing field. Harland then drove his car around the edge of the football field to the tunnel on the opposite side of the stadium and left unscathed, except for his pride.

The stadium manager went out and told the crowd to go home.

"We're waiting for Harland," a few of the angry mob responded.

"Harland's gone," said the manager. "I let him out the back way."

The crowd then began throwing things at the stadium manager until the police dispersed the crowd. That was Harland Svare's last appearance as the Chargers' head coach.

Coach Ron Waller—Out of the Frying Pan, into the Fire

Ron Waller, our special teams coach, took Harland's former position as head coach for the Chargers. We called Ron by his nickname, "Ratman," a nasty-sounding name that actually was meant to be a compliment. Ratman earned his nickname for his legendary "do whatever it takes" attitude as a coach, which included spying on opposing teams and generally sneaking around like a rat.

A week after Ratman's promotion, the Chargers went to Denver to play the Broncos in Mile High Stadium. Ratman ordered a mandatory team dinner at the hotel. All the coaches, players, training staff, and equipment staff gathered to eat. Everyone showed up—even the bad boys, who were usually out until bed check.

Dinner was buffet style, and everyone went through the line and began to eat. There was very little conversation between the players—many were focused on tomorrow's game—just the sound of silverware clinking on plates. Most football players took eating seriously, and mealtime usually went undisturbed. But just when the big guys were getting down and greasy, someone knocked on the door. The players paid little attention to the knocking until Ratman finally said, "Somebody, see who that is."

Jimmy Hammond, the trainer, was closest to the door. He jumped up and opened it to the irate mugs of two Denver policemen. Everyone stopped eating and stared at the police. Throughout the room, several faces appeared to have something to hide.

"Come in. Can I help you?" Ratman said.

The policemen stepped into the room, looked around, and settled their sights on Tim Rossovich and Dave Costa. "We received a complaint that those two removed a telephone from the Playboy Bunny Club," one policeman said.

Ratman sighed deeply. He was very familiar with the team he'd inherited. "Tim, did you do it?" he asked.

Tim hunched his shoulders and shook his head.

"Dave, did you do it?" Ratman continued.

Dave lifted his hands out, as if to say, "who me," and shook his head.

"Unless you have evidence, officer," Ratman said, "it looks like there's been some mistake."

"I'm sorry to interrupt your dinner," the policeman said. But he continued to look around the room, as though searching for anything suspicious. Knowing what Tim and Dave were capable of, I was certain that this wasn't the end of it.

With everyone watching, Ratman walked the policemen to the door. Just before they opened the door to leave, Tim pulled a red telephone out from under his shirt and yelled, "*Rinnnnnng.* Officer, somebody wants you on the phone." He began swinging the telephone over his head. "Anybody want to make a long distance call?" he shouted.

The room exploded with laughter. One of the officers confiscated the heisted phone, warning Ratman, "Control your men unless you want to play a game without them."

Ratman's head coaching position with the Chargers turned out to be so challenging that he sought divine intervention. After the policemen left, Ratman looked as if he been handed the last regiment from the Looney-bin for a team, and his men were out of control. Not that there weren't any seriously ambitious football players present. Most of the team was determined to win each game they played, but a few rebels like Costa and Rossovich were causing Ratman's hair to go prematurely gray.

Before our team meeting later that night, Ratman sent Jim Hammond—known as "Hambone"—on a mission to find a black Baptist minister to come and pray with the team and "preach to them the old-time religious gospel." I guess he figured a rousing threat of fire and brimstone would create some desire in his poorly performing team to make a good showing. That in itself was a joke. At that hour on a Saturday night, the prospect of finding a minister was unlikely, but Ratman knew he needed more than he had to offer to fire up that bunch he'd been left with.

The team gathered at the usual hour for the meeting, but Hammond hadn't yet returned. After a long wait, Hammond burst through the door and said, "God damn, you ain't going to believe this, but I ran into this chick in the lobby and damned near married her. I forgot all about the preacher."

The team burst out in laughter. Surely, that fired the team up more than a preacher would have. Cat calls, whistles, and barks of, "Go get 'em, Bone," rang out.

"Calm down, calm down," Ratman ordered. "I'll do it myself." He made a humble effort to secure some blessings for his unlikely bunch with his own plea to a higher being—finishing his prayer with, "Lord, forgive these trifling, no-good, mother-f--ing thieves, for they are misfits."

Ratman's speech must have fired Rossovich up. He hardly ever said anything, but on the way out to the field the next day, he yelled, "Let's burn the barns and take their women." But we went out and got our butts kicked, 30-19, and headed back home to San Diego. Ratman's tenure lasted but six games, as the Chargers promptly let him go at season's end after a 1-5 finish to the year.

It Must Be the Shoes

On the football field one Sunday in Denver, a thin coat of ice made for treacherous footing. Everyone was slipping and sliding, especially the players running downfield. Yet Gary "The Ghost" Garrison, a three-time All-Pro receiver, was able to stay on his feet each time he ran downfield to catch a pass. This drew the attention of the field judges.

While on the sidelines, he was wearing the same regulation shoes that I'd issued him. But when he went on to the field, he wasn't wearing the same shoes. Gary had exchanged his regulation shoes for spikes when he went in for a play. His accomplice was fellow receiver Chuck Detwiler, who had Gary's regulation shoes ready for him to switch back into the minute he sat on the bench. As for me—I pretended not to notice.

After a couple of plays, one of the officials came to our bench and asked Gary to show him the type of shoes he was wearing. A player could be thrown out of a game for wearing non-regulation shoes, especially spikes used for track. Upon inspecting Gary's shoes, the official shook his head in wonder, and told Gary his shoes were okay. Gary continued to play with spectacular grace and form, planting his feet exactly where he wanted to, so much so that at halftime the official came to our bench and again asked to see Gary's shoes. And once again, the official concluded that they were okay.

"Sir," Gary asked the official, with the most puzzled look he could muster, "is there something wrong with my shoes?"

"No," the official replied. "You have amazing balance out there. I don't know how you do it."

Gary looked over his shoulder at Detwiler, who was hiding the pair of spikes, and then back to the official. "That's why they call me the ghost," he said.

A Life-Endangering Threat

During the time Don Coryell coached the Chargers—the "Air Coryell" days—for every away game Dan Fouts, Charlie

Joiner, Kellen Winslow, and I left the hotel on game day at 9 a.m. sharp. Mind you, riding with me to the stadium every Sunday was their idea—not mine. I don't think it was that they loved my company so much as they loved getting to the stadium early enough to engage in a little game of dominoes before the kickoff. They were supposed to ride the bus with the rest of the team, but no, when my cab pulled up, there they were in the back seat: Kellen sitting behind the driver, Charlie in the middle (because he was the smallest), and Dan behind me. Each week the seating arrangement was the same.

One week before a game against the Seahawks, our cab picked us up at the appointed time. Cloaked in a Northwest downpour, this Sunday morning in Seattle was a depressing, soggy, sunless day. To take our minds off the weather and the upcoming contest, we joked about who the best domino player was while discussing the scores of the college games from the day before. We always paid close attention to the college scoreboard. The NFL—despite having a wide range of big and small colleges represented in the league—had only one Air Force graduate in tow: me. If Air Force had lost that week, I wouldn't say anything; but if they won, just to rub it in, I would say, "Didn't Air Force win yesterday?"

On this day, I asked that very question. One of them unfolded the sports section of the newspaper and pretended to check the scores. "There is no mention of Air Force in the news," he told me. "Are you sure they have a team?" The three of them laughed. Shortly thereafter, the cab pulled up to the gate at the stadium, and the guard stopped us.

"You'll have to let them off here," she told us. "Cabs drop off their fares here at the entrance and turn around. I'm sorry, but the cab can't go in."

Our laughter faded. The gate was about a block and a half from the entrance to the indoor stadium, and it was still pouring rain. No one made a move. Each time we'd played in Seattle before, the cab driver had been allowed to take us right up to the door of the visiting locker room.

"What can we do, Doc?" Dan asked. The rain seemed to dare us to step outside and face a drenching. We certainly weren't daring each other. None of us had any intention of walking the rest of the way in the rain. The guard folded her arms across her chest and glared. I didn't doubt that she knew who we were, just as I didn't doubt that it wouldn't have made a difference if I'd told her.

"Yeah, Doc," Charlie said. "What can we do?"

I thought for a minute, reached inside my bag of tricks, and came up with one of my incredible inventions, which I called necessary inventions. After all, I was not just the issuer of jocks, but "the Doc"—the go-to-guy, Mr. Fixit, and protector of my team. I dropped my voice to a whisper, and adopted the desperate tone of a frightened man. "You've got to let him take us in. We need to get in there without being seen. The detective told us to come early because there's been a threat on the lives of these players. You don't want to have to live with being responsible if something happens to them, do you?"

The guard threw up her hands and jumped back from the window, reacting to my news. "Go on. Get in there now," she demanded. "Hurry up. Just go."

The cab took off, and we quickly filled it with laughter. "Doc," Charlie said, laughing so hard he could hardly get the words out, "you amaze me. Where did you come up with that one?"

"Don't ask," Kellen said. "Let's just run with it."

Could You Give Us a Push?

Usually, my cab trips on the road with Dan, Charlie, and Kellen went smoothly—guards or no guards. But on one occasion, the excursion became troublesome. Snow had fallen all week in Minnesota before we arrived there for a game. The roads in the area—covered with ice—had slicked up like greased glass, and I was just happy to have someone else doing the driving. The cab we rode in made good progress until we were within about 200 yards from the stadium's front entrance. The driver accelerated to go up a small hill, and the tires spun in place. There we sat, spinning our wheels until the cab began sliding back down the hill, skidding from side to side. All of us were white-knuckled.

"Let's see if we can go around the back," Dan told the driver. "We can get out where the delivery trucks unload."

The driver tried to turn around by putting the car in reverse, but it spun out again, pitched, and did a little rock and roll before ending up with its rear backed up against an iron post. No one said much. We were all staggered by the turn of events. The driver switched from reverse to drive to make the turn for the back entrance, but that only buried the tires deeper into the ice and snow.

"What is Coryell going to say when he finds out three of his starters and the equipment manager are stuck on an icy hill and rammed into an iron post?" Dan wondered. "What if we had gotten hurt?"

"You're not hurt," I said, "and if he asks me, I'll tell him I was asleep. So, Kellen, one of you can tell him what happened."

"He'll probably ask about you first, Doc," Kellen said. "To hell with the rest of us."

"You guys are full of it. You're in my cab, you know," I reminded them.

In the end, the four of us climbed out of our seats and pushed the car off the small hill. The guys in the back seat had a game of football to play, I had 40 guys to dress, and we were out in the stadium parking lot pushing a cab. No one saw us— thankfully—or we would have probably read about it in the newspapers the next day. We got back in the cab and the driver let us off at the loading dock.

Forty-five minutes later the rest of the team arrived. My riding partners whistled like boiling teapots. Kellen chirped loud and long about our dilemma. Even Charlie, who hardly ever said a word, couldn't wait to tell everyone the whole story. They blamed me when things went wrong on the way to the stadium—rain, snow, ice, whatever. Having them with me meant I could count on being the whole team's source of humor for the day. I was like the big brother they could do anything to and I wouldn't get mad. But they all knew I'd get even, which could be counted on. Calamity and fun followed when I was with those three, and there was always more to come.

Pops

On one of our trips to Kansas City to play the Chiefs, I followed my early Sunday morning routine and arranged for a taxi to pick me up in front of the hotel at 9 a.m. sharp. Of course, Dan, Charlie, and Kellen came along for the ride. When we arrived at the stadium there were broadcasting trucks blocking the entrance to the tunnel, and the locker room was a quarter of a mile away. The temperature outside had dropped to freezing.

"Ok, Doc," Dan said. "It's colder than a well digger's behind out there. You mean there's nothing we can do to get the cab down the tunnel and take us to the locker room?"

"The snow's stopped," I said. "Suck it up."

"We'll get you for this," Dan said, as if hitching a ride in my cab entitled them to complain and harass me.

We walked, and upon reaching the end of the tunnel, a left turn led us to the visiting team locker room. As usual, a locker room guard sat near the door. We walked up to him laughing about something that had happened in Friday's practice, and I guess maybe he didn't like it when the opposing team came into Kansas City with smiles on their faces. When I passed him, I said, "Good morning, Pops," trying to be friendly in a familiar way. I didn't mean to insinuate that he was old. I'd spent many of my teenage years in St. Louis, Missouri, where jazz music and the slang of the era became a part of my young experience. The term "Pops" was only a greeting to another man, regardless of age. Without a thought about it, that old slang came to mind. My hair had turned as white as an Alaskan blizzard, and the guard was about 20 years younger than I.

Before I could add the words, "how are you doing," he stood up, reared back, and with a growl in his voice, said, "Who are you calling Pops, you old motherf---er?"

Taken aback, I stammered, "I'm sorry, young man." Out of the corner of my eye I saw my companions double over, not even trying to muffle their snickers. That was one of those moments when I wished I could have snuck away. Those guys already had one on me and the day was just getting started.

As soon as I got in the locker room, I knew the fodder was going to fly. Sure enough, Charlie waited by the door and greeted the rest of the players, repeating the scene. Each time I passed one of the players in the locker room, he said, "How are you doing today, Pops?" A reenactment of the event went on and on in the training room. Kellen chalked his hair white, and Dan narrated. Soon, everyone knew just how it had gone down. The players passed the guard on their way out to warmups and asked, "Have you seen that old guy that called you Pops?"

"No. I haven't seen the old motherf---er," he said, adding fuel to the fire. That incident loosened the team up. I went out the side door to the playing field after all the players had left the locker room in order to avoid seeing the guard and risk a reprise. We won the game, and by the end of the day I could smile along with all those who had teased me. I even tipped the guard outside our locker room. I gave my younger enemy an extra 20-dollar bill. He pocketed the money and thanked me. As I walked away he yelled at my back, "Hey, Pops, have a good trip home."

Who Took My Cab?

Doug "Moosie" Wilkerson, our big offensive lineman, also didn't like waiting for the team bus to take him to the stadium when we were on the road. He usually followed Dan, Charlie, Kellen, and me to the stadium in a cab of his own. On one Sunday, Ed White, Don Macek, and Russ Washington took Moosie's cab before he could make it downstairs. They knew Doug would react like a mad bull, but those guys were always stirring up trouble just to incite a reaction. The cab they took followed behind our cab. Soon we heard an announcement over the car radio to all cabs. "There's a big, black man back at the Chargers' hotel mad as hell because someone took his reserved cab. We told him someone with the same name had claimed the reservation."

You can imagine the laughter that erupted in our cab. We couldn't wait until Moosie showed up at the stadium. Ed, Donnie, and Russ got to the stadium and waited for him to arrive. When they heard him coming—fussing all the way in that high-pitched voice of his (which made his ranting all the funnier)—they ran to the toilets, closed the doors, and pulled their feet up on the seats so Moosie couldn't see them.

Moosie was always serious on game day, and he never wanted to speak to anyone. But that day he came into the locker room blowing steam. "Where are they? Where are they?" he screamed. He marched through the locker room, his fists clenched. Someone started laughing in the toilet area. Moosie heard the laughter, turned, and went to his locker, his anger now giving way to the humor of the situation. Don, Russ, and Ed slinked out of the toilet stalls, and soon everyone was back in game mode.

A Long Hot Day in Miami

In 1981, we went 10-6 to make the playoffs. We headed to Miami to face the Dolphins with a trip to the AFC championship game on the line. Team owner Eugene Klein took everyone in the organization to the game, including the secretaries, the coaches' wives, and his friends. My wife let our youngest son, Brett, take her place.

On New Year's Eve, EVK threw a party for the team. The offensive linemen were not known for their fashion sense, but Ed White had come prepared to party. He'd done an appearance for Munsingwear back in Minnesota. Leisure suits were going out of style, but Ed accepted a dozen leisure suits in every color of the rainbow as compensation for his appearance. For the party, all the offensive linemen and Dan Fouts dressed in the suits.

Two days later we played in the longest game in Chargers history, a thrilling game that ended after nearly 14 minutes of overtime after we kicked a field goal to secure a 41-38 win. The players were all beat up, dehydrated, and running on adrenaline. Doug Wilkerson pulled a bench into the showers, and the linemen flopped on the bench and let the shower water cool them off. The defense, meanwhile, collapsed in a corner of the locker room.

One sports writer interviewing the players after the game asked Louie Kelcher, "How do you feel?"

"I feel like I rode a horse from San Diego to here," Louie said.

The same reporter then asked White the same question. "I feel like I was that horse Louie rode here on," said Ed, speaking for the rest of the team.

The Hot Seat

Before each away game I called the city we were traveling to in order to get the weather forecast for that weekend. Before a scheduled game in Cleveland, the weather forecast predicted "severe cold." I mentioned the weather to Mr. Klein, and told him that a Mr. Jenkins in New Jersey had designed an electric hot seat to keep players warm on the sidelines. I suggested that we look into getting one for the game.

"Get it," he said, without asking how much it would cost. I never volunteered to tell him that the cost to rent the bench for a game was $5,000. On the Saturday night before the game, the temperature dropped as forecast. Coaches and players asked, "Did you get the bench, Doc?"

Of course, I had already lined it up.

"Why did I ask you? I knew you'd have it," coach Dave Levy told me, shaking his head.

Then on Sunday morning, before pregame warmups, Coach Levy and the offensive linemen went out early. A short while later Bob Wick, my assistant, came running in to tell me that Coach Levy wanted to see me right away.

"Do you know what he wants, Bob?" I asked.

"No, but he said he needs to see you right away."

I went out to see what Dave wanted. He was standing by the bench, which had steam drifting up from its hot seat. All of a sudden, the temperature in the stadium must have risen to 60 degrees, erasing the need for any added warmth.

"What are you going to tell Eugene V. Klein for getting the bench on a warm day like this?" he asked me.

"How did I know the weather was going to warm up? Anyhow, what bench?" I gave him the blankest look I could muster. "I don't know what you're talking about."

"My mistake," Levy said. "I guess we don't have that bench." He pointed to the steaming hot seat, a smile crinkling his face.

I called the grounds crew and we hid the bench in the basement of the stadium, out of sight. I had authorization to use it, but I knew I'd be the laughing stock of the team if I left the bench out there on the field for all to see. I asked Mr. Jenkins, the owner of the seat, if he'd wait until the end of the game before he took it away, and signed a contract to that outcome.

Coach Levy couldn't wait to tell Fouts and the offensive linemen that I'd hid the bench. No one said a word more to me about it, but Dan couldn't keep a good thing to himself when he had something on someone, especially me. Sure enough, a week later the entire line stood before me wearing T-shirts that read, "SOB—Save Our Bench and Doc's Job." They rode me about that for some time, but in the end they knew that they could count on me if they ever needed anything—even a hot seat.

Scary Reflections

Louie Kelcher and Gary Johnson were good-spirited roommates on the road that had a lot of fun together. But on one particular road trip to St. Louis, Louie got to enjoy himself a bit more than Gary. Louie and Gary checked into their hotel room, a room with two double beds and a full-length mirror on the bathroom door. That night before the game Louie went to bed early to get a good night's sleep. At around 3 a.m. a blood-curdling scream woke Louie from his sleep. He heard heavy breathing near the foot of his bed, and quickly yelled out for his roommate. Now Louie was no lightweight at 6 feet, 5 inches and 280 pounds, and I'm probably being nice by a few pounds. Any intruder would have had a death wish to mess around with Louie, let alone Gary, who was 6 feet, 3 inches and 250 pounds.

"Gary!" shouted Louie.

"I'm here," Gary replied.

Louie quickly turned on the light to find Gary standing at the foot of his bed.

"What's wrong?" Louis asked.

"I got up to go to the bathroom," said Gary, "and when I got near the door, I saw this big, dark man coming at me with no clothes on."

"What did he look like?"

"I didn't wait to see."

Louie looked at Gary—standing their shaking, as naked as a newborn—and then at the mirror on the bathroom door. "Go back to the bathroom," Louie said.

Gary headed for the bathroom, and his image grew larger as he neared the mirror.

"You see him now, don't you?" Louie asked, about to crack up.

Gary covered his eyes in embarrassment. "Don't tell anybody, man," he pleaded. "You'd better not tell a soul."

"No, Buddy," Louie said. "You're my roommate. What happens in this room stays in this room." Louie covered the mirror with towels to avoid any more disruption, and headed back to sleep.

The next day when Gary showed up in the locker room, all the players, one after the other, passed him and patted him on the back, asking, "Any big naked men been after you lately?"

6

COACH TOMMY PROTHRO

A Wise Man

A cigarette often hung between the middle and index fingers of coach Tommy Prothro's right hand as though it were a permanent appendage. Between drags he spoke in long, slow drawls through a fog of heavy smoke. "Sid," he told me, dragging out my name so that the "I" in it went on and on, "if you're ever in need of anything, and the Chargers won't help you, come to me." I liked him immediately.

Coach Prothro wasn't a big talker, however. I had overheard former head coach Harland Svare deliver pleading speeches to the players before games in order to get them to shape up. And Ratman would curse them and call them misfits. But Prothro topped them all in his speech prior to our first game of the 1975 season. That team that included rookies Gary Johnson, Mike Williams, Louie Kelcher, Fred Dean, Ricky Young, Billy Shields, Ralph Perretta, and Mike Fuller. Coach's speech was surely memorable for those young guys preparing to face the World Champion Pittsburgh Steelers at home before a sellout crowd in their first NFL game.

The team gathered for the Saturday night meeting, anxiously awaiting to hear what coach had to say. I'm certain that there wasn't a dry armpit in the room. Time passed and finally Coach Prothro entered the meeting room. He puffed continually on a cigarette, and paced in front of the guys for a few minutes. A man of few words, he finally spoke the words they waited to hear. "You know," he said with a long, southern drawl. "On your best day you couldn't beat this ball club." He turned and went back to his room.

"Man, I'm pissed!" Louie Kelcher said. "We'll show that old fart." And on Sunday they did. The Chargers kept the Steelers under 40 points, losing to them 37-0.

Coach Prothro was a wise man.

Always Playing Games

In 1974 the Chargers hired a new head coach, Tommy Prothro, who had an eye for talent, good instincts, and a competitive spirit. Prothro's successful draft in 1975 marked the beginning of an upward swing for the Chargers. Many of the players he drafted that year became a key part of the Super Chargers teams of late '70s and early '80s. But Prothro also loved a challenge off the field as much as he loved football. He was just a gamer, as they say. As soon as he walked into the locker room, he would join the players in whatever board games they happened to be playing: chess, checkers, bid whist, backgammon, or dominoes.

Coach challenged Ed White to a game of backgammon every day before practice. The locker room would fill up with smoke, with gamblers on one side and non-gamblers on the other. Ed claims Prothro still owes him five bucks, but he doesn't know how to collect it now that Coach is calling plays on the other side. Coach absolutely hated to lose, so if Ed won the game, Coach would yell at him extra loud during practice that day.

On the road Prothro had me arrange the seating on the plane according to the games: domino players in one section, bid whist players in another, and chess players in yet another section. The games were played in tournaments with the winners advancing to the championship game. He said the games taught strategy, defense, and aggressiveness. He loved the competitiveness of the games, especially chess, where Ira Gordon was his strongest opponent.

Non-Crisp Toast
and No-Heat Hot Cakes

Prothro was fanatical about food. Unfortunately Bob Hood, the business manager at the time Prothro was head coach, was in charge of meal planning at home and on the road. Bob's nemesis became pregame meals, because no matter how hard he tried, he ended up with his tail tied in a knot. Bob swore the last person you wanted to be around during pregame meals was the head coach—not just Prothro, but any head coach. The coach was nervous, his players were nervous, and whoever got in the way of either was made whipping a boy.

During one of these pregame breakfasts, Prothro, miffed in his un-hurried way, asked Bob how he ordered the toast. He addressed Bob as though his first and last name was hyphenated like Billy-Bob or Jimmy-John, and elongated Bob's surname so that it lilted on and on. Bob didn't want to answer that he'd obviously ordered for the toast to be toasted, so he responded, "without butter."

"Bobby-Ho-o-o-d," Prothro said, "Well it's not crisp. Toast should be crisp. Look around this room at all these players eating non-crisp toast. It takes too long to digest. Some of their careers are on the line. If they get sick on the field and can't play football, you're responsible. What are you going to do about it?"

"Well, Coach, in the future, I'll see to it that they get crisp toast," Bob replied. He then walked over to the table where the team doctors were eating, and sat down with them. "How many of you learned in medical school the length of time it takes crisp toast to digest versus non-crisp toast?" Bob asked. "Because if some of the players get sick out there today, my ass is toast." The docs laughed and laughed, but Coach's talk had already made its impact on Bob. (By the end of that season, Bob thought he'd be better off cooking the meals himself.)

The following week the Chargers had a road trip, and if Bob had thought that the crisp toast incident was a bad dream, he had yet to face his worst nightmare. Coach Prothro told Bob he wanted to change the pregame meal.

"How do you want to change it, Coach?" Bob asked.

"Well, I think the players ate too much at the last pregame meal," said Coach. "Some of them ate like it was the last supper, and you know, for some of them, it was."

"What do you want me to do about it, Coach?"

"I want them to sit down to a meal," Coach responded. "Just bring them a plate of food, and that's all they get. They can have a choice of pancakes and eggs, waffles and eggs, or hamburger and eggs."

"Coach, we're going on the road this week. How are we going to arrange this, and how are we going to decide who gets what?" Bob wondered.

"On the way up on the plane, you take orders," Prothro decided, thus turning Bob into a waitress, and a frustrated one at that. The nightmare only worsened, however. On the morning before the game, Prothro told Bob that he wanted to change who could attend the pre-game meal. He only wanted coaches, players, and the doctors to be present. No other staff members were allowed. "And that includes you," he told Bob.

"But, Coach, it's my job to be there to make sure everything goes smoothly," Bob pleaded. "I *have* to be there."

"I want you at the bottom of the stairs to keep everyone else out. Send them to the coffee shop. We'll pay for their breakfast, but I don't want any distractions." Breakfast began at 9 a.m. on game day. About 30 minutes later, smoke began to fill the restaurant; waitresses scurried back and forth in confused urgency. Just as Bob began to really get worried, Bobb McKittrick, one of the assistant coaches, came down the stairs and said, "Bob, you'd better get up there."

"He doesn't want me up there," Bob said, speaking of Coach Prothro.

"Go up the back stairs and do something before we get thrown out of here or the place burns down," pled McKittrick.

So Bob snuck into the dining room through the back door. Complete chaos had overtaken the room. Players didn't remember what they'd ordered on the plane, and when one saw what was on the other's plate, he wanted that. The waitresses were running around in circles, changing plates and canceling orders. The kitchen was burning hamburgers in an attempt to keep pace. No one was happy, and then Prothro spotted Bob. "Bob-by Ho-o-o-d," he said. "Come over here." Prothro was seated with a plate of pancakes and eggs in front of him. Bob knew he was going to be chewed out royally, but he sucked it up and went to face him. Prothro continued, "Put your hand on these hot cakes."

"Huh?" Bob said.

"Put your hand on these hot cakes."

Bob laid his hand on top of Coach's pancakes and quickly removed it. He didn't want his hand on Coach's food.

"Do you feel any heat?" coach asked.

"No, Coach."

"Well, how can they be hot cakes with no heat?"

"I'll speak with the kitchen, Coach."

Poor Bob. Nothing got past the attentive ears of the players when someone was put on the spot. Bob had to endure teasing—"Do you feel any heat?"—for weeks to come. But even worse was that Prothro made Bob Hood feel the heat on every road trip.

Reversed Fortune

Coach Prothro drove a golf cart from one group of players to another during practice, for instance, from defense to offense to special teams. He would pull his cart up to one group, stop, and get out. After he'd worked with that group, he'd hop back on the cart and go on to the next group. He left the cart idling while he was talking with each group, and the cart just dozed in place until given the gas. Everyone knew that when Prothro got back on the cart that his foot came down hard on the gas pedal like a racer on the Indianapolis speedway. He rushed quarterback Cliff Olander with the cart one day and broke his leg. Of course he didn't run into him intentionally, but winning football games blinded him.

Toni Fritsch, an Austrian soccer-style kicker, was with the Chargers for one year, during which he partied hard at night. In the daytime he crawled behind the dummies and slept while the rest of the team practiced. Awakened for kicks, he went out, kicked a few balls, and then generally wandered around causing trouble.

One day Toni spotted Prothro's idling golf cart, and inspired by his overindulgence of liquid courage from the previous evening, he was overcome with a bright idea that was too good to pass up. He snuck up to Coach Prothro's cart and put it in reverse. All of us held our breath as Coach Prothro, his attention already focused on the next group of players, got back on the cart, grabbed the steering wheel, floored the gas, and went flying across the field in reverse. Prothro held on like a cowboy riding a bucking bronco—of course with a cigarette glued between his lips. No one laughed, even though everyone's sides were splitting from holding it inside. We just did our best to look at the ground. If any of us had made eye contact with each other, the whole team would have exploded with laughter.

Prothro hit the brakes, shifted gears, and puffing smoke like an old coal stove, rode off to the next group without ever saying a word. Inside the locker room, the players jumped all over Toni. "What were you doing, trying to get us all cut?" we asked. Prothro was a good sport about it: A few days later, he informed Toni that he'd be better off playing for another team.

Good for a Laugh

Coach Prothro's intensity sometimes got in the way of his common sense. One day in Seattle's dome—which was, of course, protected from outside weather—Prothro went down the sideline asking players, "Did anybody notice which way the wind's blowing?" That of course produced a lot of funny looks and a big laugh behind his back. From there, things got worse. With the offense on the field ready for third down, Coach began calling for the punt team. He was hollering for "Bensky, Bersky," or whatever sounded close to kicker Rolf Benirschke's name in an attempt to get his attention. He sent Rolf out to punt with another down left to go, alarming both sides of the bench. That wasn't funny at the time, but eventually it became a running joke, as "Punt team!" echoed throughout the locker room for as long as Prothro coached the Chargers.

Freeze!

Our longest road trip—15 days—took us to Norman, Oklahoma, for an exhibition game against New England. In Oklahoma, before his hometown crowd, Joe Washington, the Chargers' first-round draft pick in 1977, injured his knee in the first half of that game. From Oklahoma we went on to Tokyo, Japan, to play the first NFL game outside the USA, and then back to Honolulu, Hawaii. In addition to our actual games, we spent a lot of time on the plane playing other games to take up time. But long before we reached the Far East, the games had lost their appeal and the tired warriors slept quietly.

Only 15 minutes from Tokyo airport, Prothro woke me up when his voice came booming over the intercom in his slow Southern drawl: "S-i-i-i-d-ney, come to the front of the plane." Everyone awoke and craned their necks to see what was going on. Making my way to the front of the plane, I wondered, too.

"Sidney," Prothro puffed and then said through a fog of smoke. "I want you to be the first one off the plane, so you can see to it that all the bags get off the plane and are loaded onto the equipment truck. I want everything arriving at the hotel at the same time."

It had never been my job to handle personal bags, but Prothro had a knack for making everyone's job more difficult than usual. Bob Hood could attest to that; his players could, too.

Orders were orders, so after the plane landed, I got off before everyone else and headed for the baggage chute. A Japanese liaison who spoke English came to meet the plane, but he went straight to the front of the plane to greet the other passengers. That left me without a translator and armed with only two sentences of Japanese.

I started for the unloading belt, and six policemen, buckled up and booted like Kamikaze pilots, pointed their guns at me. I stopped, stuck my chest out, and said hello in Japanese. Not a bit impressed, they never blinked and kept their guns aimed at my head. I stood before them dressed in a suit and tie, my hands in the air with the August sun beating down on me, and sweat rolling down my face. From the corner of my eye I saw the rest of the team headed for the buses. The policemen didn't say a word, and I was afraid to speak again. Finally, the Japanese liaison came around the corner toward me. He spoke to the uniformed men in a scolding tone, and they put their guns back in the holsters. With new bravery, I said goodbye in Japanese to the six stone-faced police officers, just to let them know I spoke the language.

Coach Prothro held the buses up while he stopped to ask me, "Si-i-i-dney, is everything all right?"

"Yes, Coach," I answered. "Everything is all right." You could count on him to back you up.

Little Accommodations for Big Men

The Chargers stayed at the Hotel New Otani in Tokyo. The doorways at the hotel were too low, the beds too short, the players too big for that little society. We had to get extensions for some of the beds. Players without their wives shared a room with a roommate, their traveling bags, helmets, shoulder pads, thigh and kneepads, and shoes. Joe Washington, who was injured, had 12 pairs of shoes stacked in his room. Locals gawked and followed our big guys around, giggling, as if the players were circus freaks.

In spite of the novelty of big men among them, the people of Japan were kind and hospitable, and the Chargers, Coach Prothro, and the St. Louis Cardinals paved the way for all of the other NFL out-of-country exhibition games that followed.

7

RACING THE ROOKIES

Unofficial Start

My tradition of racing the rookies began one day in the parking lot at the stadium in 1975. We were standing around dropping little bits of history about each other. Joe Beauchamp, a defensive back who was nearly ten years younger than I, bragged about his speed, how he'd lettered in track at Rufus High School in Milwaukee, Wisconsin.

"You don't want me to shut you up," I said. "You can't beat 'The Rabbit.'"

My teammates from Festus High School in Festus, Missouri, had given me that nickname. I'd lettered in track there. Three other guys and I had been the state championship relay team, and we ran all the sprints, too.

"Come on," Joe said. "You want me. Let's get it on." He dropped in a starting position. "I'll give you a five-yard lead," he continued.

"When you get to the finish line," I said. "I'll be sitting down eating lunch." I hiked up my pant legs and shook my legs, snorted like a pony at the starting gate. We didn't have a gun, and Bobby Howard was laughing too hard to count, so someone else called, "Ready, set, go!" I think I took off on "set," but Joe was too busy getting ready to be beaten to notice. I came out ahead by inches, and felt good about dusting off one of the speedsters in the defensive backfield. When that bit of news hit the locker room, my stature grew, and by next year my "racing a rookie" campaign had begun.

Choosing My Opponent Wisely

By 1978, the race had become a fun event that took place annually after the last practice of training camp. The whole team looked forward to seeing one of them bested by their old equipment manager. Not being a fool, I didn't race just any rookie. By this time I was 43, and the average age of the rookies was 20. No one knew this, but each year I went to the scouts and got the name of a lineman who'd timed the slowest. He would become my opponent.

When the last practice of the 1978 training camp ended, Coach Prothro asked me, "Sid, do you want to race this year?" I had picked my victim, Milton Hardaway, an offensive tackle out of Oklahoma State. Hardaway was huge—6 feet, 9 inches, and 324 pounds with a size 17 EEEE shoe. His shoe was big enough that a baby could sleep in it. He was the "Hulk," the largest man ever drafted by the Chargers. Yet he was a musical giant who played the harmonica so well that he brought tears to his teammates' eyes. But I wasn't concerned with his musical ability; my only care was that he couldn't run.

The rest of the team lined up at the finish line along with Mr. Klein, the team owner, and his wife, Joyce. Ninety percent of the crowd was on my side; the players knew who to root for if they didn't want their jocks to itch. I came out dressed in brand new warmups with zippers on the sides of the pant legs for easy removal without taking my shoes off. Coach told Milton he was the chosen one. A rookie could—but rarely did—refuse to race me. Years later, Trent Green, a quarterback, did refuse to race me. He told me he was afraid he'd be cut if I beat him, so I let him slide.

Milton lined up, ready to take me on, and the crowd cheered. A couple of guys held the tape at the finish line. I shook my arms and legs, snorted, blew air out of my mouth, loosening up. Off came my jacket, and I unzipped the sides of my warmup pants. I wore my running shorts underneath them. What I did next will attest to how nervous I was to show my athletic ability in front of professional athletes. In my haste to get started, I grabbed the top of my pants, and not realizing that I had hold of the top of my shorts also, I pulled everything down and stood on the practice field in my jock and running shoes.

A loud cheer went up. Embarrassed that I had practically exposed myself in front of the owner's wife, who was bent to her knees with laughter along with everyone else, I hurried and pulled my shorts back up. (Kicker Rolf Benirschke slipped his camera behind him, but I knew he had already snapped the picture.) The race ensued, and I won, breaking the tape yards ahead of poor Hardaway.

"Take the lap, Doc," someone yelled. "Yeah, take the lap," others joined in. I took a victory lap, waving my hands in the air. I passed Louie Kelcher, and he yelled, "Your shorts slowed you down, Doc. You should have kept them off."

Ganged Up On

The last Charger I raced was Billy Joe Tolliver, our round-bodied quarterback, who moved about as fast as an out-of-gas lawn mower. The race took place in the stadium after the last game of the 1989 season in front of about one-quarter of the crowd that had come to see the Chargers' 19-16 win over the Broncos. When the game ended we went inside the locker room and said a short prayer. Coach Dan Henning looked at me, chomping at the bit, and said, "The race is on."

I took off my pants, already clad in my Olympic running gear. By this time, I had gotten cocky despite my aging knees and the little bit extra I was carrying around my middle. Billy

Joe took off his shoulder pads, and the team headed back to the field. Some members of the press followed us back out, too, complaining that they had to wait to interview the players.

I stretched, did a few sprints, and gave Billy Joe a sample of my crazy-leg shakes. I held a 16-0-1 record against the rookies, having tied with Dennis McKnight in 1982.

"Oh, you need to sit down, old man," Billy Joe said before the whistle blew. I snorted and pranced in front of him. When the whistle sounded, we took off, and I left Billy Joe at the starting gate. I was a lot older and a lot slower than when I'd began the races, but Billy Joe didn't turn out to be my greatest challenge. Watching him run was like watching paint peel. Billy Ray Smith and Gary Plummer held the tape, and I saw them move it as I neared the finish. Billy Ray knew that Billy Joe might not have been as fast as I was, but he'd last longer. Those Texas boys with two names played a trick on me. I ran a fixed race—the finish line constantly moving—and Billy Joe eventually came out on top. I should have stuck with a lineman for an opponent.

8

ON THE SIDELINES

Players don't always lounge on the bench—as it might seem from the stands or on TV—while on the sidelines waiting to be called to play. The sideline is where serious decision making takes place: a change of strategy or game plan, a player substitution, adjustments and repair to equipment, and the evaluation of injuries. The sideline is where the force of a collision vibrates, because the sounds are the loudest. Sometimes on the sideline the boys exhibited their need to wreck havoc in the midst of the already existent insanity. And sometimes, when the need arose, I became the team's secret weapon.

Game-Winning Touchdown

Running back Bob Thomas came to the Chargers in 1973 from the Los Angeles Rams. Bob worked hard to make the team and become a starter. Late in a Sunday afternoon game against Buffalo in San Diego, Bob got his chance when the call came for him to find the seam between the right guard and the right tackle. On the handoff, he tucked the ball under his right arm, and while fending off defenders with his left hand out in front of him he broke through the defensive line and dashed like an Olympic sprinter into the open field. He never saw the defender that hit him from the left side, helmet to helmet, and he went down hard.

A murmur of concern began on the bench when we saw that Bob wasn't moving. The doctors and trainers ran out on the field, gathered around him, and checked him out while we held our collective breath. After a while Bob stirred, and the trainers helped the wobbly-legged runner to the sidelines and sat him on a bench. His eyes rolled around in his head like dots on a spinning top.

Meanwhile the game continued, and on the next play Cid Edwards took the ball and ran 20 yards into the end zone for the score. The stadium erupted with cheers.

Still woozy, Bob asked, "What happened?"

I think it might have been Reggie Berry who slapped Bob on his back and responded, "You just won the game with that 35-yard run you made. They're yelling for you. Give them some love. Wave, man. Wave to your fans."

Bob stood up and waved. The crowd responded as if Bob's wave were an announcement that he was okay, and they cheered louder. This reinforced Bob's belief that he'd scored a touchdown, and the headache squeezing his head like a tight drum didn't seem so bad. Then Reggie went up and down the bench and told the entire sideline to go over and tell Bob what a hell of a run he'd made for a touchdown. The team poured the praise on so thick Bob might have thought he'd been selected to the Pro Bowl.

After the game, the doctor—who was on the same page as the team—examined Bob again. "You got hit pretty hard before the touchdown," he told Bob. "You may have a headache for a few days, but I don't see anything serious. Congratulations on the score."

Bob went home to Los Angeles and came back to San Diego for the team meeting on Monday, at which time the team always reviews the videotape of the previous game. Everyone waited for Bob's big play—knowing that Bob was still unaware of the part he *didn't* play in winning the game. The film rolled. Bob saw himself go down on the field, and the play that followed. His jaw dropped, and his chin pointed to the floor. The room exploded with laughter.

That was his hazing. Welcome to San Diego.

A Greasy Slip

In any game, the chance of undisputed All-Pro defensive tackle Louie Kelcher being outplayed at the line of scrimmage was unlikely. Yet in one particular game, that's exactly what happened; he kept getting beat at the line of scrimmage. When the offense took the field after a rough defensive sequence, Louie came to the sideline, wringing his big hands and looking puzzled.

Jerry Smith, the defensive coach, yelled at him: "Louie, what the hell's the matter with you? It's ass-kicking time. What's going on out there?"

"That guy's holding me, and the ref's not calling sh-t," Louie replied.

He wandered over to where I was, stood next to me, and said, "God that's it, Doc. What can we do about the guy holding me?"

"Don't worry about it," I said. "I'll take care of it when you go back in."

"How can you take care of it?" he asked.

"Just do what I tell you," I said.

A moment before the defense went back onto the field, I opened a jar of Vaseline and slopped the entire jar on Louie's hands. His hands were so big, that it took a whole jar to cover them.

"Let him hold you on the next play," I told him, "and you grab his jersey and slide your hands down it. Rub the Vaseline over him and then call the referee. Tell him the player has something slick on his jersey. Show the referee how the stuff has come off on your hands."

Having any slippery substance on a uniform was against league rules, and grounds for removal from the field of play. I was hoping this trick would help get Louie free to return to his normal self. The center snapped the ball, and before the quarterback could step back, the same lineman grabbed a hold of Louie. Louie ground his hands into the man's jersey just as he was told, and slicked him up like a buttered roll. Then Louie approached the referee when the whistle sounded. "That man has something on his jersey," Louie said. "See how it got all over my hands."

The referee took a look at Louie's hands and then at the man's jersey and asked the player from the opposing team to leave the field and not come back until he'd found a clean jersey. We didn't see that offensive lineman again for an entire quarter while his equipment people scampered to find a replacement jersey for him.

Louie came back to the sideline smiling. "Doc, you know all the tricks," he said. "I bet he won't hold me again."

I gave Louie a startled glance. "Who me? What tricks? I don't know what you're talking about."

Standing in front of a misting fan with sweat dripping down the sides of his face, Louie swatted me on the back with a mighty blow and laughed. "That's why you're the man, Doc."

Schmoozing with the Zebras

I've always believed in the old saying, "You catch more flies with honey than with vinegar." Anyway, in my day I knew about 90 percent of the referees; most were good people that I honestly liked. I made an effort to learn everything I could about them: their names, their hometowns, their wives' names, et cetera. You never want a referee as your enemy, as they simply had a lot of influence on the outcome of a game.

Three days prior to every NFL game, the league sends a memo to each team with the names of the officiating crew for the upcoming game. We were especially interested in the refs prior to a game against the Raiders, a team that could be counted on to play dirty and try to get away with as much as possible.

In this particular game, Dan Fouts stepped back from the huddle, pumped the ball right, and then released it in a high spiral to Wes Chandler. Wes' hands were as sure to hold as tacky glue. He turned to go back for the ball, and a Raider player stuck his foot out and tripped Wes as the ball sailed past him. No flag was thrown. In a moment of anger and frustration, coach Dan Henning yelled at the field judge, "Hey Ref!" But the ref wouldn't acknowledge him.

I went to the coach and told him, "That referee's name is Tom and if you want him to listen to you, address him by name."

Later in the game the same referee threw a flag against one of the Chargers' players, and Coach Henning spoke to him by name as though they were old friends. The referee came over to talk. That talk didn't change the call, but it helped Henning get the referee's attention when the game wasn't going his way.

"Hey, that worked, Doc. How do you know all their names?" Henning asked.

"You're better off if you don't know," I said, winking as I walked away. I went down the sideline and spoke to another referee, "How are you, John? How're the kids?"

It pays to know your friends *and* your enemies.

Seeing Yellow

The Chargers came away the victor in one of the epic games in NFL history at the 1982 Orange Bowl against the Miami Dolphins. The players gave it their all in the 41-38 overtime victory. Later we read a comment in one of Miami's newspapers from a Dolphins player who claimed that Kellen Winslow—who had suffered from exhaustion and dehydration in that game and had to be literally dragged off the field—should have received an Academy Award for his acting ability. He claimed that Kellen faked his extreme burnout. That comment ticked our team off more than a little bit. That's when the so-called bad blood between the Chargers and the Dolphins began. The Dolphins would never again be safe in Chargers territory.

I was ready for them the next time they traveled to San Diego. I used some of my tactics to throw their rhythm out of sync. I knew every rule in the official rulebook concerning the sidelines. One rule states that a player can have nothing on his person on the playing field that simulates a flag. The Miami Dolphin players went out on the field of play wearing orange gloves. The orange wasn't even close to the yellow of the flags, and I knew it. But I still went to the official and complained, "Our players are confused by the gloves Miami players are wearing. The gloves look very much like flags."

The official told Bobby Monica, the Dolphins' equipment manager, to have the Miami players remove the gloves until halftime. The outcome may not have been the result of the loss of their gloves, but Miami receivers dropped balls the rest of the first half. At halftime, Monica took off like a greyhound to get the rulebook. Shortly afterwards, one of the referees called me to the official's locker room and showed me the rule in the book. I told him I knew the rules but the gloves appeared yellow to our players, and were causing confusion. Monica came back on the field after halftime holding the rulebook above his head like Moses with the Ten Commandments for me to see. I didn't care. The Chargers were winning. I laughed and laughed.

Beating Them with Their Own Game Plan

All's fair in love and war, which made any type of warfare in the game of football legitimate. Jerry Glanville and his Atlanta Falcons came to San Diego to play the Chargers two weeks after he appeared on ESPN. On TV, Glanville demonstrated how he gathered his team in a huddle on the sideline before each game, reached in a predelivered box, extracted a replica of the opposing team's helmet, and instructed his players to beat up the helmet before kickoff. Fortunately for us, I'd tuned in to the show that day and was ready for him. The S.I.A. (Sid's Intelligence Agency) went into action to make sure that trick didn't happen when the Falcons played the Chargers.

We stationed an S.I.A. person—namely, a ball boy—to watch out for the box. Sure enough, after pregame warmups, one of the Falcons assistants brought out a box, like the one I'd seen on TV, and sat it between the two benches on the visiting team's sideline. My man's assignment was to watch the box. The Falcons assistant went back inside and came out a few minutes later with a bag, went over to the box, and put a helmet in it. The S.I.A. agent had his eye on the assistant the whole time and watched him go back through the tunnel to the locker room. We stationed another agent outside the tunnel to serve as lookout, just in case the Falcons assistant happened to come back out before we finished our mission: to replace the Chargers helmet with a Falcons helmet.

Our agents—five ball boys, all die-hard Chargers fans who weren't about to allow their team any embarrassment they could prevent—went to work. One agent swapped the helmets and placed the stolen Chargers helmet in a Wilson football bag used to transport the game-day footballs. He passed the bag to another agent standing at the south end of the field, who then passed it on to another as a cover. Then that S.I.A. agent headed toward the official's locker room to make it appear that he was taking footballs to the officials, when they were really discarding the stolen helmet. Everyone employed under the equipment department knew his job was to help the Chargers win by any legal means necessary, and some might have gone a little further if asked.

The Falcons came back out to their sideline before the start of the game, and Coach Glanville gathered his players around him in a huddle, reached into the box, and lifted the helmet over his head within the players' reach. The Falcons charged, grunting, like hungry dogs after a piece of meat, and commenced to slap the helmet as if to destroy it. Realizing, after a few seconds, that the helmet they were attacking was their own, their hands dropped and their faces soured. Glanville stomped, threw the helmet back in the box, and snapped his head back and forth from one side of the field to the other, searching for culprits. He then began ranting at his perplexed equipment people for the mix-up.

Meanwhile, the S.I.A went back undercover. Posted from one end of the field to the other, agents for the Chargers wore smiles as secretive as happy thieves and acted unaware of the Falcons' troubles.

I saw Coach Glanville after the game, and fed him a clue. "Have a safe trip home, Coach," I said. "You looked real good on TV."

I imagined him halfway home—finally realizing the error of his loose lips—sitting straight up in his seat on the plane and declaring, "Well, I'll be damned."

Hold Card

Ball boys-turned-S.I.A-agents worked the visiting locker room, the tunnel, and the sidelines. They were trained by the spy master—me—and they employed a wide range of weapons and tactics. For example, on his way out to the playing field, an opposing team's quarterback might misplace his four-inch wristband with all his plays on it. A well-trained S.I.A. agent might find the wristband and transport it back to the Chargers locker room. Soon enough, S.I.A. Headquarters, otherwise known as the Chargers coaching staff, would call the locker room looking for intelligence concerning the opposing team. They knew my agents were always on the lookout.

The visiting teams used a blackboard in their locker room to go over plays during half time. Routinely, one of the team members would erase the blackboard before heading back out to the field of play. But on occasion, the blackboard wouldn't be erased, and the information on it would be seized by well-intended undercover agents. On several occasions, our visiting locker room attendant discovered a blackboard loaded with information. He turned the blackboard around, hiding the goods, and then smeared chalk over the side facing out to give the appearance that the board had been erased. The next morning we took pictures of the blackboard and passed the information on to headquarters to use when we met those unsuspecting gentlemen again.

Once I found a book of plays and play calls from a team. I went over the plays and stored the book away. A year later the team played the Chargers at home in San Diego. The offense for the opposing team had the ball. I stood between Dan Fouts and James "Shack" Harris on the sideline and told them what the first three plays would be. They laughed. "Sure, Doc," Dan said.

"You'll learn to trust me," I said. "If I tell you a gnat can pull a plow; hitch him up."

The quarterback took the snap from the center, and the first play went just as I had called it. I had both of those guys scratching their heads. The next play followed my prediction as well. They looked at each other, eyebrows raised, and then at me. "No, Doc, you got lucky," Shack said. When the third play went as I'd predicted, Shack and Dan turned to each other, their faces lined with humor. Dan smiled and didn't say anything. I strutted away with my chest stuck out, as if I'd done something special.

The next morning Shack asked me, "Was that something you learned in the military?"

"If I tell you," I said and winked, "I'll have to sack you six feet under."

Bumble Bees

In 1996 the Chargers played the Steelers in Tokyo, Japan. Starter, the official NFL sporting goods company for 12 NFL teams including the Chargers, had designed a new shirt for each team. The shirt Starter made for us was white with gold gussets under the arm that resembled a bee flying when the arms were raised. "We can't stand on the sideline looking like bees," I said. While I knew we had to wear Starter shirts during the game, I came up with a plan to solve the problem. I purchased cheap white shirts, cut the labels out of them, and sewed Starter labels on them. Even the players laughed at the ugly shirts.

NFL properties asked where I got the white shirts. They were sticklers for authorized NFL merchandise.

"They're Starter shirts," I said. "Look inside." I opened the neck of one of the shirts and showed him the label. "Now do you believe me? We will not wear those bumble bee tees."

I got us out of it for that game, but back in San Diego, we had to wear those winged shirts.

Doc—Not M.D.

The players called me "Doctor," or "Doc" for short. That began when I professed to being a "Dominologist," a specialist when it came to the game of dominoes. One Sunday afternoon during a Chargers game, Burt Grossman, a defensive end with the biggest mouth to come along since Howard Cosell, went down on the field. The temperature in San Diego that day had risen to a 100 degrees, and sometimes a few minutes of rest did much to revive a player on a hot day. Burt, who was also a pretty good actor, took advantage of the opportunity.

The referees called a timeout. Keoki Kamau, our trainer, and two of our team doctors went out to check on the extent of Burt's injury. After about 45 seconds, the doctors went back to the sideline, and Keoki asked me to join him on the field. I grabbed my bag of tools, prepared for an equipment problem, and ran out on the field. I kneeled down next to Keoki and Burt and asked if something was wrong with Burt's equipment. Burt was lying on the turf with his eyes closed, his feverish face bathed in perspiration.

"Nope," Keoki said.

"Why did you call me?" I wondered.

"Burt's not really hurt," Keoki said. "The doctors checked him out. He's just hot and woozy from the heat. I called you out so he could rest a little longer. You're his alibi."

Unless a player goes down with a serious injury, he has to leave the field of play as soon as possible. So I was buying Burt some additional time. After about a minute, a referee came over and said, "I've got to start this game. You've got to get him off the field."

"We'll have him up in a second," I said, pretending to adjust his equipment.

Keoki said, "Time's up Burt." Burt had been resting with his eyes closed, but he'd been listening to everything. He opened his eyes, looked at me, and then turned to Keoki.

"Why didn't you call a doctor?" he asked.

Keoki pointed at me. "I did. He's 'The Doc.'"

"Oh, my God, 'Doc' my ass," Burt groaned. "I need a doctor and this is what I get. You guys are full of sh-t. Get me off this damned grass."

I could see that he wanted to laugh because his acting ability hadn't fooled anyone except the referees and the masses who had come to see the Chargers play. Keoki and I left the field with Grossman between us; one of his arms draped over each of our shoulders. The crowd cheered. We kept our faces straight and serious until we dumped Burt on the bench, and all three of us doubled over laughing.

"Cry wolf, Burt, and you end up with the 'Doc,'" Keoki said.

Crap Happens

Sometimes real mishaps occurred on the sideline. Murphy's Law dictates that anything that could go wrong would go wrong, and sometimes we were unprepared for the truly unexpected. We were preparing to play the Raiders in the 1980 AFC Championship game. Hank Bauer, a tough little Chargers running back nicknamed "The Howitzer" because he hit so hard on special teams, did not appear to be his usual fired-up, let's-go-get-them self. He stared off in space and stood quietly with his right hand gripping his mid-section while the team captains went to the center of the field for the coin toss. Meanwhile, Hank, shivering on the sideline, had turned the color of chalk.

The team captains came off the field and one after the other slapped Hank on the back and said, "It's Howitzer time." The special team players gathered around the coach to go over their strategy to stop the Raiders' kick return man.

"Hank, are you ready?" the coach asked.

"I am, Coach," Hank said, failing to inspire any confidence. You would have thought that a nest of hornets had taken up residence inside him, the way he clutched his gut. I expected him to tell the coach he was sick, but he gripped his middle and moved lead-footed to his position. The Chargers got set and, at the whistle, Rolf Benirschke kicked the ball into the end zone. The Raiders' kick return man caught the ball and returned it to the 28-yard line, far beyond the point the Chargers had hoped to contain him.

Hank hit him and they both went down as if they'd been hit with a twice-by-heavy, known in the lumber yard as a two-by-four. Despite his size—5 feet, 11 inches, and 210 pounds—Hank was the special teams hit man against whom all others were measured. I had never before seen The Howitzer tackle anyone and go down the way he did. But he did make the stop.

Still, Hank came off the field shaking his head. He knew he had not made a good enough play. When Hank made a good hit on a player, he'd come off the field and stand by the coach. This time Hank went to opposite end of the sideline bench, away from the rest of the team. A little while later he called me, "Doc, I need to see you."

"Are you okay?" I asked.

He shook his head and looked at me with pink-veined, tired eyes. "I was sick last night and I just got the shit knocked out of me," he responded.

As I got closer the wind shifted, and I knew he was telling the truth—literally.

"Can you help me, Doc? What should I do?" he asked.

Players did not leave the field in the middle of a game except in an emergency, and this was the first crisis of that nature that I had come up against. The only equipment that I knew of that could help Hank's predicament was a shower and clean clothes. I threw him a towel from as close as I dared to get.

"I can't help you," I said. "But you can do two things. The first one is to wrap this towel around you." Hank was only wearing a jock under his pants, which didn't afford much leeway for an accident of this nature. "Go to the locker room, and change your uniform. Be sure to shower. The second thing you can do is get the hell away from me."

He laughed when I said that.

"I'll talk to coach," I said. "Just go."

"Why is Hank walking like that? Where is he going?" one of his teammates asked. "Is he alright?"

"Don't ask," I said. That secret was between Hank, the coach, and me: Even on the sideline, crap happens.

Lifting Our Voices

On the sideline Louie Kelcher and I won the contest for the singing voices most likely to offend listening ears. Neither of us could carry a tune. Recently, I received a note from Louie that read, "My best memory of game day on the sideline will always be the opportunity I had to sing the "Star Spangled Banner" with my special buddy, Sid "Doc" Brooks. I still get misty-eyed and chills around my expanding middle when I think back and see Doc step forward to hit "the rockets' red glare" with me, and see tears in the eyes of everyone around us from the pain of it. I will never forget it."

Neither will I.

What You See Is Not Always What You Get

The Chargers prepared to play the Steelers on a Sunday afternoon in Pittsburgh during the 1984 season. Our wide receiver, Charlie Joiner, was just one catch away from breaking Charley Taylor's NFL career record of 649 receptions. Charlie was going to get that catch before the game ended. We all knew that. As was customary, football players who made a special play in a game could keep the football that was in use at the time of the play. Record-breaking balls went to the Pro Football Hall of Fame, and there was no question where Charlie's ball would end up.

I took my usual cab ride to the stadium that day with Dan Fouts, Kellen Winslow, and Charlie. And also as usual, Dan and Kellen were ribbing me about something.

"The bet's on that you'll get the ball before Charlie catches it," Dan said to me, referring to the special ball that was going to the Hall of Fame.

"You mean Doc's going to catch the ball?" Kellen asked.

"No," Dan said. "I mean Doc will be on the field to get it before it warms in Charlie's hands."

The backseat erupted in laughter.

"Quit messing with me," I said, and laughed too. "You're going to throw it to him, right?" I lifted my eyebrows at Dan with the question.

"I'm going to throw it to him at some point," Dan said. "I know you'll have your eyes on the ball at all times, but I'll give you a signal. When I slap the top of my helmet in the huddle and look away from Charlie, that's your cue."

"Don't sweat it, Doc," Charlie said. "If I catch that ball, I'm going to give it to you. It's yours to do with what you want."

When the offense left the sideline to take their place on the field, Dan said, "Doc, are you ready?"

I was ready, but cool Charlie Joiner was more nervous than anyone imagined. Charlie was always quiet, but on this day he was more silent than usual. The Pro Football Hall of Fame people waited on the sideline for the ball. The players knew they were there, but they kidded me about substituting the actual ball and giving the Hall a dud. I wouldn't do that, would I?

It was the fourth quarter and late in the game when Dan slapped his helmet, looked away from Charlie, took a step back, and fired the ball over the middle. Charlie slipped behind the defensive line like a shadow and snatched the record-breaking catch before the Steelers had time to react. The referees stopped the game to acknowledge Charlie's achievement, and I ran out on the field to secure the ball before the whistle quit blowing. I took it to the sideline and placed it beside another one that Charlie had caught from Dan earlier during warmups. When the Hall of Fame people came to collect the record-tying football, I reached down, picked up one of the balls, and handed it to one of them. Who has the real ball? Only the equipment man knows for sure.

Gotcha!

Dan Fouts picked on me constantly; that's how I know he would have been lost anywhere else in the league without me. But on at least one particular occasion, I learned that I would have been lost without Dan as well.

At a party at linebacker Cliff Thrift's house, tight end Eric Sievers tried to drown me by throwing me into the deep end of the pool. (I couldn't swim.) Dan, knowing the loss he'd face without me, jumped in and saved me after I'd gone down for a second time.

I credit him with saving my life, and I owe him. With deep affection, I know, and a magnitude of mischief, he defrocked me on the sideline in Chicago during a Monday night game. I always dressed the team to impress, and on this Monday night I dressed myself to match. After the game got underway, the TV announcers commented that, "Only two people on the field are wearing ties tonight—Ditka, the head coach for the Chicago Bears, and Sid Brooks, the equipment manager for the Chargers."

Moments later Dan stood in front of me with the trainer's scissors in his hand.

"You're wearing a tie, huh?" he asked, before clipping my tie off to a nub before I could even duck. With my teammates laughing along with me, I removed what was left of the tie and my white dress shirt and slipped into a coach's polo shirt.

"Now you can take that butt down off your shoulders and get down with the rest of the men," Dan said.

I already had. I never wore a tie on the sideline again.

Don't Mess with the Fashion Police

The Chargers dressed for a game in the best-looking uniform in the league. I saw to that. I purchased and laid out gameday clothing in such a way that when the Chargers took the field, they were, in my opinion, looking good. Sometimes a fashion expert on the team had a different opinion and wanted his attire his way. I had means to make them understand that it was my way or no way without them ever knowing that I'd changed their minds.

One Sunday, I checked everyone over as usual—coaches, ball boys, doctors, trainers, and players. When my eye reached Larry Pasquale, the special teams coach, I saw that he had tucked his jacket into his pants. I approached him and in my most diplomatic voice said, "Coach, your jacket is not outside your pants. You'd be more in uniform with your coat on the outside the way everyone else does it. I want you to look like the pro that you are."

I don't know why anyone ever listened to me, but most of the time everyone did. He was watching a play on the field and didn't answer. I waited until the play ended and reminded him again of our dress rule. He looked at me as if to say, "How dare you tell me how to dress."

"Okay," I said to myself, "I'll show you what I mean." I went to our trainer, Keoki, and asked for a scalpel. He gave me a number fifteen blade, sharp enough that the slightest slash with it would cut through skin, flesh, and muscle.

"What do you need a blade for?" Keoki asked.

"I'll show you at the end of the quarter."

The play ended and the special teams players gathered around Coach Pasquale. I went behind him, hardly making a sound, and with a single surgical motion, sliced his jacket in two with that number fifteen blade from top to bottom. The jacket fell open like a ripe watermelon. I was surprised that the rush of air that escaped the jacket didn't cause Pasquale to notice. A few minutes after the beginning of the second quarter, one of the players went to Coach and said, "Your jacket is open in the back, all the way down."

Pasquale took off his jacket, examined it and asked one of the ball boys to place it on the bench. Keoki had been watching the entire episode. He bent over near the bench, laughing. I returned the blade to him and he said, "You showed him what to wear one way or the other."

After the game Pasquale brought his jacket to me. "Look what happened to my jacket, Doc. Do you think you can fix it?"

I examined the jacket with the most puzzled expression that I could conjure up without laughing out loud. "Funny that it would come apart like this," I said. "No problem. I can fix it. Damn companies don't make clothing like they used to."

The next Sunday Pasquale wore his jacket outside his pants. Nobody messed up my wardrobe on the sideline and got away with it.

Raining Ice Balls from the Stands

The equipment man, well-equipped but not suited out, is seldom injured during a game, but I turned out to be the exception. The date was December 23, 1995. I won't forget the date because December 23 is the date I married my wife. It was my anniversary. I was thinking about her that cold day of the regular-season's finale at the New Jersey Meadowlands. Heavy snow fell the night before and well into Sunday. The field had been cleared, but the cold, wet, white stuff remained piled high in the stands. The Giants had struggled through a miserable season, and many of the regular-season ticket holders had opted to stay home by the fire, selling or giving away their tickets, while disgruntled, rowdy fans drank beer and filled the seats.

The Giants were losing, and fans began pelting the field with ice balls, iced rock-hard with beer and whatever else they could find. When the people in the stands started aiming the missiles at the officials, I went to get help from security, and that's when I went down.

The next thing I knew a lot of people were standing over me. "Don't move. Let me get the blood out of your eye," Keoki said. I was on the ground. Defensive end, Chris Mimms stood over me with his cape tenting me from further attack. I held my hand up so my wife could see the two rings I wore on my ring finger. I wanted to sit up so my family would know I was okay. NBC's Will McDonough thankfully announced that I was awake and calling the ice-ball throwers a few unfavorable names of my own.

I was not okay, but for the moment I was alive. None of us knew then that I'd be on medication for the rest of my life to treat the seizures caused by the scarring on my brain from the trauma. A few inches here or there might have blinded me or proven fatal. I was lucky. I received numerous letters from the NFL, the Giants, the Meadowlands, and from fans around the country, especially ones from New York, apologizing for the behavior of a few, who they assured me were not the norm. I want fans everywhere to know that no game is worth someone's life—that football is a game of sport where NFL players shake the hands of their opponents when the game is over like gentlemen.

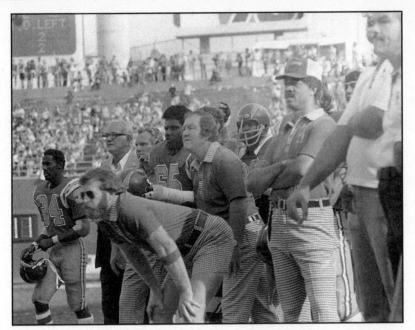

Standing on the sideline during the Tommy Prothro era in the mid-'70s. The pants (and shorts) were in style, then. *Photo by Gene Leff*

(Left to right) Dan Fouts, Charlie Joiner, me, Ahmad Rashad, and Ed White pose for the camera prior to a game. *Photo by Bob Redding*

Deacon Jones made it clear from Day One that he had my back, which helped to make my transition from the Armed Forces to the NFL a smooth one.
Photo by Sporting News Archives/Icon SMI

Coach Don Coryell stands on the field prior to the start of a 1979 pre-season game against the 49ers. Coryell led us to the playoffs that year for the first time in over a decade.
Photo by Michael Zagaris/Getty Images

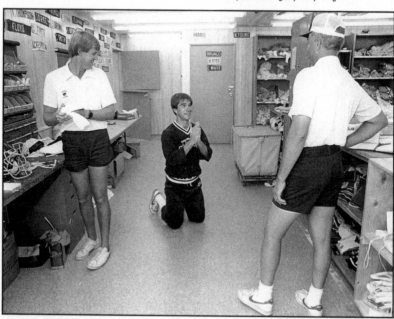

If you entered "The Dungeon," as we called the equipment office, you'd better be nice to the dungeon rats. Defensive line coach Gunther Cunningham is down on his knees pleading for some coffee as my assistant, Bob Wick, looks on.
Photo by Sam Stone

Louie Kelcher and I pose at Fred Dean's wedding. Fred had all his best men wear their uniforms, and had me dress as an official. *Photo courtesy of Sid Brooks*

Pete Lazetich, known for his oddly shaped head, tries on the "watermelon helmet" trainer Rich McDonald and I made for him. *Photo by Gene Leff*

Kicker Chris Bahr receives the "Gold Card" T-shirt from me after being elected the Player of the Week by the dungeon rats. Gold Card recipients received priority in the locker room and training room, and plenty of other perks, including a limo ride to and from the stadium. *Photo by Sam Stone*

In the locker room, no one was safe from a good-natured joke. I pose with Ed White, who went by the nickname "Wide Load," and the refrigerator we dressed up to resemble him. *Photo by Sam Stone*

Quarterback Sean Salisbury wore this jersey through an entire practice without realizing that we had purposely misspelled his name on the back. *Photo courtesy of Sid Brooks*

Players gather for their postgame treatment: lots of ice and lots of ice-cold refreshments. From left to right: Doug Wilkerson, Bob Thomas, Dan Fouts, me, and Ed White. *Photo by Sam Stone*

Doug Wilkerson (right) reacts to a speech by Chargers owner Eugene Klein after San Diego defeated Denver 17-7 in 1979. *Photo by Andy Hayt/Getty Images*

(Left to right) Charlie Joiner, John Jefferson, and Kellen Winslow on the sideline during a 1980 game against our rivals, the Raiders. *Photo by Michael Zagaris/Getty Images*

Pete Shaw hands the football he caught for his first career interception to my assistant, Bronco Hinek, as Kellen Winslow looks on. *Photo by Sam Stone*

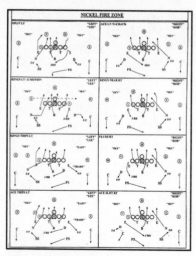

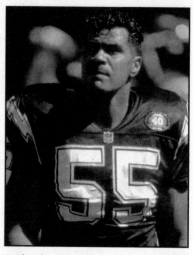

A confiscated page out of our opponent's playbook. We used our ball boys—members of Sid's Intelligence Agency, or the S.I.A.—as spies. In the NFL, if you're in enemy territory, always make sure to empty your trashcans. *Courtesy of Sid Brooks*

Linebacker Junior Seau pauses during a game. Junior, who was around for my final 11 seasons with the team, was a wonderful teammate and community member. *Photo by Sam Stone*

The "ball" which Charlie Joiner caught to tie the NFL's career record for receptions. *Photo courtesy of Sid Brooks*

Dominos were the No. 1 pastime in the Chargers locker room. Here I make my grand entrance—led by Charlie Joiner, carrying the championship belt—during my championship match against offensive lineman Dennis McKnight. *Photo courtesy of Sid Brooks*

McKnight (center) makes his entrance, surrounded by his posse, (left to right) Ed White, Russ Washington, and Billy Shields. It's hard to believe, but this domino match was featured on national TV during halftime of a Saturday night game between the Chargers and 49ers. *Photo courtesy of Sid Brooks*

The "honor guard" for the big game—(left to right) Gary Johnson, Woodrow Lowe, Leroy Jones, and Louie Kelcher. *Photo courtesy of Sid Brooks*

At "the boneyard"—as we called the domino table—with my corner man, Charlie Joiner. *Photo courtesy of Sid Brooks*

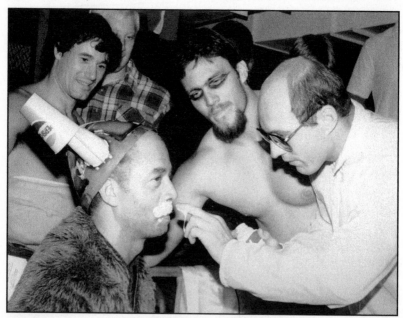

I didn't lose often, but on this night I did. The stakes of the game: the loser says goodbye to his facial hair. Hank Bauer shaves off my mustache, as McKnight and his goatee look on. *Photo courtesy of Sid Brooks*

More action at the boneyard. This time my opponent is quarterback Ed Luther, as James "Shack" Harris looks on in the background. *Photo courtesy of Sid Brooks*

They called me "The Doc"—as in "Doctor of Dominology"—for a reason: I defended the title belt on a regular basis. *Photo courtesy of Sid Brooks*

San Diego Padres superstar Tony Gwynn hands me the ball after I threw out the first pitch at a Padres game in May of 1999. *Photo courtesy of Sid Brooks*

Chargers head trainer Keoki Kamau and I pose for a photo prior to a game. We had a good run together in San Diego. *Photo courtesy of Sid Brooks*

There was plenty to gain by schmoozing with the officials. Here, they return the kindness by posing for a photo with me prior to my last home game with the Chargers. *Photo by Sam Stone*

9

DOMINOS

Welcome to the Bone Yard

The oldest known domino dates back to 1120 A.D. and is believed to be of Chinese origin. But the Chinese would never have imagined the bone-slapping, mouth-yapping game played around various NFL locker rooms. In the Chargers locker room, the language of dominos was a speech all its own. "Let's go to the bone yard" was an invitation to play. When you were at the table and a game was in progress, you were at the bone yard. "Give me fever" meant 5 points were scored. "Ten halt Texas" translated to 10 points. "Give me 15 stitches in a hobo's britches" was the slang for 15, and "highway 20" was the imaginary highway that led to anyone's hometown and meant 20. "A deuce and a quarter Buick" stood for 25. "I'm thirsty" was code for 30, as in, "When I get to St. Louis (the name of your opponent's hometown) I'm thirsty."

Talking smack was as much a part of the game as the numbers a player slapped on the table. Every domino player on the Chargers team played against me at some point, but only a few ever beat me. I picked opponents I knew I could crush, and then

I talked big. "I'll give you 50 points just to sit down," I would say before starting a game to 300.

One trainer, Steve Roccereto, who had never played dominos but had watched silently and studied the game, beat me with white knuckles and sweat dripping down his face. The players wouldn't let me forget it. If I began to brag, someone chirped in, "Alright, Doc, I'm going to get Steve in here to shut you up."

But despite all the smack talk, the domino games were about belonging, about friendship. Because of the games, our team was close.

The Daily Foursomes

My opponents changed many times over the years. I called myself a Dominologist, a doctor of dominology. Of course there is no such thing, but the name stuck. At the end of my career players were calling me Doc and Doctor without knowing that the nickname started as a result of dominos.

While we were all together in San Diego, quarterbacks Dan Fouts and James "Shack" Harris played doubles with Charlie Joiner and me every Wednesday, Thursday, and Friday before the morning meeting. It was a good way to start the day. On Sunday mornings before home games, Dan came in at 9:30 a.m. to get partially taped, and then he and I went to the quiet of Whitey's kitchen and played dominos for a half hour. Whitey Weideman was a longtime Padres affiliate and cooked for the Padres. Sometimes on weekdays we'd eat his chili while we played dominos. After our game, Dan went back to the locker room, studied, and put his game face on.

During the week we were a foursome. Dan was wise and witty, the intellectual. Charlie played a serious game and laughed at everything. He had to laugh, because Shack was the ultimate funny guy. Shack stopped each day at the grocers, bought a bag of black grapes, and ate them while we played dominos, all the while telling stories about his days at Grambling just to make us laugh. My favorite college story of his was about him being named MVP of a football game *at half-time*; he watched the second half from the stands, sitting beside his mother. He had hundreds of stories like that.

Bones in the Smokehouse

Playing dominos was addictive. In the off-season coach Ernie Zampese, photographer Gene Leff, Coach Jackie Simpson, and scout Red Phillips—another foursome—slapped bones in the small coaches lounge from 8 a.m. to 4 p.m. like men spending a day at the office. They puffed away on tobacco sticks while making the bones rattle. The smoke in there was so thick you needed a flashlight to find your way from one end of the room to the other.

All Night Long

Some members of the team played dominos non-stop, so much so that a rumor went around the locker room that guys were taking a shower pill so they wouldn't have to stop the game for the real thing. One Thanksgiving, practice was over early so everyone could spend the rest of the day with families. I left a handful of players rattling bones. I told them to turn out the light when they left. I arrived at work the next morning at 6 a.m. to find Leslie O'Neil and Stanley Richard still playing. I can't say for sure if they'd been at it all night, but chicken bones *were* piled in the trashcans.

Stumped While Cameras Rolled

I played a championship game against offensive lineman Dennis "Conan" McKnight. Dennis came by the nickname "Conan" after the lead character in one of his favorite movies, *Conan the Barbarian*. The stakes were high for our match—my mustache for Dennis' goatee. Hank Bauer stood by with a razor in hand and a grin on his face, knowing that he was going to take pleasure in being the executioner of someone's facial hair. The domino shootout was featured on national TV during halftime of a Saturday night game between us and the 49ers, with sports analysts Merlin Olsen and Dick Enberg handling the announcing. I had talked up the match, and with the buildup the whole team, coaches and players, showed up in festive regalia to see if Dennis would be the one to be beat me.

On Friday after practice, in a big production, I dressed in a green fur jacket and a Viking hat with horns. My warriors—Louie Kelcher, Woodrow Lowe, Leroy Jones, and Gary Johnson—came out to support me wearing only towels around their lower halfs, bearing baseball bats, an American flag, and singing the National Anthem. Charlie acted as my manager. He sat in my corner and guarded me. Dan Fouts sat inside the ring as the commissioner. In as much as I was the doctor, I prepared to operate. My get-up was designed to scare Dennis into losing, and to heighten the mood of the show I used all the tricks I had at my disposal. Rick McDonald, the trainer asked if I needed Valium.

"What for?" I asked. "I'm going to take him to the cleaners before he knows he's dirty."

Dennis had a few tricks of his own. Escorted by the offensive linemen—Ed White, Russ Washington, and Billy Shields—Conan had blackened his eyes, bared his muscular chest, and tied a red band around his long black hair. Kellen Winslow was his corner man, supplying him with water and wiping his brow after the game got underway. Wes Chandler manned the camera. We took our places across from each other and shook hands. The bones hit the table, and I settled back in my seat. The room got so quiet that you could have heard car tires rolling down Friars Road.

With all the lights and attention on me, I probably could have used something to calm me down. Yet my nervousness only showed in the outcome of the game: Dennis won.

The second half of football began, and the cameras from the crew covering the football game rolled in for a close up of me. Merlin Olsen said, "Oh! Oh! What's different about the doctor? He's lost his mustache to Conan. Sid and the players have a great relationship."

I lost my mustache, but the Chargers won the game. That's really what mattered to us.

Many Contestants Along the Way

Coach Dan Henning had instructed everyone to report in at seven in the morning the day after Thanksgiving to witness the big domino game against the Doctor of Dominology and defensive back Vencie Glenn. The players gathered and Coach announced, "Vencie has been strutting around telling everyone he is the champion domino player. Today he is going to prove it."

One of the players brought a table and placed it in the middle of the room. Someone else placed two chairs at the table across from each other. Mr. Marker, Leslie O'Neil, gave us two minutes to get ready. I shook with Vencie like a boxer touching gloves before a match, and went in the back room. A few minutes later I emerged in a tux. This was going to be a formal killing. Everyone laughed and cheered while Vencie shook. His terror only increased my confidence. Vencie lost that game the minute I walked into that room.

Once the bones rattled, Vencie never knew what hit him. He could play, but that day he never got in his game, and I played like a man who couldn't lose. For weeks afterwards everyone called me "The Hustler," the Jackie Gleason of dominos.

Big Threat from a Big Cat

We called him "Big Cat," and at 6 feet, 9 inches, and 320 pounds, Ernie Ladd was just that. A former defensive end for the Chargers in the early '60s who had gone on to become a star in the World Wrestling Federation, Ladd's bellowing voice was just as formidable as his size. One day, in the course of training camp, Big Cat stood in the door of the locker room and cast a shadow across the room as humongous as a mountain. "Where is that so-called Doctor of Dominology?" he shouted. "Tell him he can't run from me. I'm here to shut him up. Tell him to come on out and challenge the Big Cat."

Confronted by not only big Ernie Ladd, but also his friend, notorious wrestler Andre the Giant, I was the one doing the shaking this time. The Giant towered over me by nine or ten inches and appeared to weigh a ton. I couldn't run; the game was on. It was lunchtime, and some of the players set up a game table and chairs outside under some trees. They gathered around in a circus atmosphere, all of them in my corner. Ernie's only ally was The Giant. I feared no one in a domino game, but Big Cat spooked me when he lifted all seven of his dominos in one of his mighty hands. For the first time in my life I was afraid in a domino game. But I stayed, I played, and I won.

A year later, on a television interview before a wrestling match, Big Cat bellowed, "Sid Brooks, I'm coming back to beat you. You better be ready." The camera closed in on his face, menacing and threatening, and then he winked.

"Come and get me," I said (to the TV screen).

Retraction

On occasion, when I played singles in a domino game and it appeared that I might lose, I found a way to be mysteriously called away by an emergency. I never admitted it at the time, but that didn't stop some players from suspecting things weren't on the up and up. Quarterback Billy Joe Tolliver accused me of ducking him, that is until I finally gave him the sort of licking at dominos that a young whippersnapper like him deserved. He took those words back in writing by penning a retraction in the *San Diego Tribune*. To quote Billy: "I take back what I said about Doc being a Doctor of Duckology. He stopped ducking me and played me an entire game of dominos and won. Sid Brooks is the Doctor of Dominology, and I'm man enough to say so. One day I would love to walk in his shadow."

Who's Your Daddy?

I represented the Chargers at the draft when the team selected Junior Seau in 1990. I hadn't seen him since that time he snuck into the Chargers locker room—then just a high schooler—in order to touch Dan Fouts' helmet. Junior Seau became a first-class, ten-time All-Pro linebacker with the Chargers, but he also enjoyed rattling the bones. He challenged me to a game of dominos nearly every day during my last ten years with the Chargers. We played dominos in the morning at 6:30 a.m. Our stakes: the loser had to refer to the winner as "Daddy" for the rest of the day.

One day, after Junior lost to me, I went up to him on the sideline while the team warmed up for practice. "What's my name?" I asked him.

He scanned the area around us before he answered in a mumble, "Daddy."

"What did you say? I didn't hear you clearly," I retorted.

"Daddy," he responded, a bit louder. By this time our ribbing had caught the attention of other players. Realizing what was going on, they began to laugh.

"Say it like you mean it," I said, egged on by the attention we drew.

"Daddy!" he yelled.

Satisfied, I walked away, still the Doctor of Dominology. As for Junior, he still calls me "Daddy" to this day.

10

PRANKS

The Committee

Every member of the Chargers was subjected to the pranks played on him. Coaches, players, scouts, and ball boys all felt the sting of being had. We formed a pranks committee. In the beginning the committee consisted of James Harris, Dan Fouts, Charlie Joiner, Ed White, Pat Curran, and me. After a lot of begging we let Kellen Winslow in as a junior honorary member, and Hank Bauer got in as "Mr. Baldy."

To some members of the team, I was considered to be the mastermind behind the pranks. But I beg to differ. Off and on during my time with the Chargers, some of the world's greatest pranksters passed among us. Supposedly, one person could not play a trick without committee approval, but sometimes a committee member put one over on another member.

Since there was a lot of pressure on the team to win games, practices, meetings, injuries, and cuts created a high level of nail-biting tension. Bringing laughter to the locker room kept that tension at bay. Play was necessary, and after some embarrassment maybe, appreciated. Most pranks were done to teach a lesson, which usually translated to, "Don't mess with the committee."

Gullibility Where You Least Expect It

Ball boys were gullible. We knew that. Pulling a joke on a ball boy was my way of toughening them up, enabling them to laugh at themselves, which made them stronger and more confident. Each season the players couldn't wait to get one over on the ball boys. The training room was off limits to ball boys during preseason summer camp unless one was sent there on an errand. One day, I pretended to need some adhesive tape from the training room. I asked the ball boys for a volunteer to go to the training room and get the tape. All of them raised their hands, because the opportunity to step inside the training room—a forbidden territory—was so rare.

I selected a ball boy who idolized Dan Fouts, knowing that Dan was on the training table getting treatment at that time. I sent the ball boy to Jim Hammond, the trainer who was in on the joke, to retrieve the tape. Hammond told the boy he was too busy to give him tape and that he was to ask a student trainer to assist him. The student trainer gave the ball boy a roll of tape and told him not to come back asking for more. "That's the last roll we're giving that damned equipment department," the student trainer shouted.

The boy turned and glanced at Dan lying on the training table as he headed back to the locker room. Dan reached out and stopped him. "Could you help me out? I really need you to do me a favor," Dan said.

The boy's eyes lit up. Dan Fouts had touched him and now he was going to do a favor for the quarterback. "Okay," was all the youngster managed to say.

"Would you get a bucket, fill it with steam, and bring it to me?" Dan asked.

"Where's the bucket?" the kid asked, eager to please.

"Ask one of the trainers to give you one."

Dan half closed his eyes, hardly able to contain himself. Everyone else kept working as though Dan's request was everyday business as usual. No one cracked a smile. The trainer produced a bucket and proceeded to demonstrate to the ball boy how to fill the bucket with steam from a moist pack heater. When the lid was lifted on the heater, the boiling water gave off a spray of heavy steam. The trainer held the bucket and showed the ball boy how to shovel steam into the bucket with his hand, making big scooping motions. He then left the boy to his task.

The boy scooped for about two minutes and still didn't have any steam in his bucket. But he kept at it, determined as ever to fill his bucket with steam. A rookie football player began helping him in earnest, which really caused everyone to look on in amusement. The ball boy held the bucket, and the rookie fanned steam into it. Both of their faces dripped from the spray of constant moisture. Players on the tables stopped to watch, and the trainers who weren't in on the joke began to do double-takes. No one could believe that a football player actually thought he could catch steam in a bucket.

When the prank began, about 15 players were in the training room. Word spread fast throughout the locker room about the amazing feat going on in the training room, and in the end, about 50 team members stood around the two steam collectors cracking their sides laughing. At this point the ball boy was off the hook; the rookie had stolen the show. He was asked, tongue in cheek, to collect steam for the rest of the season.

Top Secret Interview

Jim Hanifan was an offensive line coach with Don Coryell. Understandably, an assistant coach is flattered when other teams recruit them for their head-coaching vacancy, and Jim was no exception. One day he received a call while at work in the coaches' office. The call went like this: "Dominic Frontiere here. I'm going to be in town on business and would like to talk to you about becoming the head coach for the L.A. Rams."

We imagined Hanifan with his hand over the receiver looking around to see if anyone was listening. Teams have to have permission to discuss a position with a coach under contract with another team.

"Strictly confidential," the caller said. "Brief meeting to set up interview. Would like to meet with you 8 o'clock Saturday morning. Is there a coffee shop nearby?"

"I don't know of one," Hanifan said.

"How about Pernicano's restaurant at 6 o'clock Saturday evening then?" the caller suggested.

"Okay," Hanifan responded before the caller hung up.

The quarterbacks and offensive linemen went to dinner at 6:30 p.m. every Saturday night before a game. The Saturday night before Hanifan's secret dinner meeting, they went early to Pernicano's, arriving at 5 p.m. to wait for Hanifan. A few minutes before 6 p.m., Hanifan showed up in a suit and tie—rare dress for him. To his surprise, he was greeted by his linemen—Ed White, Don Macek, Billy Shields, and Russ Washington—as well as quarterbacks Dan Fouts and James "Shack" Harris.

"All dressed up for an interview, huh?" Shack asked him. The others burst out laughing.

"Goddamn it, you got me," Hanifan said.

"Well," Dan said. "Since you're stuck with us, I guess that means you're buying dinner."

Who's the Turkey Now?

A flyer was posted in the locker room each year two days before Thanksgiving. The flyer stated that one of the local grocers was giving away free turkeys to the team for Thanksgiving. Team personnel had only to go to the grocery store, pick out a turkey, and identify himself as a football player or coach with the Chargers. Many of the coaches and players headed straight for the grocery store as soon as practice was over, only to be told that they'd been had. (The store was in on the prank.)

On one particular occasion, Joe Beauchamp chose his turkey, and then decided to buy a roasting pan to fit his 22-pound gobbler. Arrogantly strutting his stuff, he went to the checkout stand with his turkey in his hand hoisted above his shoulder like a waiter carrying a tray. "That'll be $20," the cashier said.

"Oh, no," Joe said. "You don't understand. My turkey is free. I'm with the Chargers."

"I don't care if you're with the Padres," the cashier said. "The only turkey in this store is you."

The next year, as Thanksgiving drew close, the veterans told the rookies not to fall for the turkey prank, attempting to ruin the equipment personnel's little joke. Well, you had to be smart to outsmart the old pro. I sent one of my guys to a Vons grocery store, and he bought a turkey and borrowed a butcher's jacket from the store with their logo on it. The name Carlos was sown on the pocket. We borrowed a volunteer from Service America, the stadium food service group, to pretend to represent the store. Doug Wilkerson was the team player's rep, and we convinced him to go along with our prank. After practice, the Vons imposter presented a turkey to Doug in the locker room in front of the players and coaches.

"Go to the Vons on Mission Gorge and tell them Carlos the Butcher sent you," our pretend Carlos told the rest of the team. "You can choose any turkey up to 20 pounds like the one Doug has. I guarantee free turkeys for everybody."

Players and coaches scrambled to get to the store and be first in line. We planted Gene Leff, a cameraman from the Chargers' video department, in the store to film the team picking up their turkeys. Sam Williams became hostile upon being denied his free turkey and loudly demanded to see the store manager. He knew the turkeys were free to the Chargers, because Doug had been given one. The store manager finally agreed to give him one just to quiet him down.

Coach George Dickson told Coach Dick Corey he could have his turkey. Dick called his wife and told her not to buy a turkey, because he was getting two free ones. He went to Vons in North County where he lived and they told him that store was not giving away free turkeys to anyone. He then drove 45 minutes back to the Vons in San Diego only to discover that he'd been duped.

In the morning meeting the next day everyone denied falling for the prank. Many players who swore they would never fall for that trick again weren't about to fess up. But Gene Leff let the film roll, and the house broke up with laughter.

Eugene Klein, the team owner, found out about the joke and the following year arranged for a ham and turkey to be delivered to everyone in the locker room. Some of the players donated theirs to the needy. Football players have big hearts inside their rugged exteriors, and had a way of turning a joke on them into joy for others.

Some Never Forget

Chip Myrtle had been in the league for several years and was no stranger to pranks when I tricked him with the turkey scam in the mid-'70s. Chip's heart was so filled with generosity that when he left the Chargers he sent me a card every year at Thanksgiving. In 1999, 25 years after he had left the Chargers, I received a very thoughtful handwritten card from the former linebacker. The content of his letter follows:

Dear Sid,

It was with some sadness that I read and heard on TV of your upcoming retirement at the end of the 1999 football season. Although I only played with the San Diego Chargers for about half of the 1974 season, your smiling face and friendship I will always cherish. Thank you very much. Walter Payton passed away yesterday, which reminded me of what's important in life. For me it's God, family, and friends. Sid Brooks fits right in with family and friends.

Meanwhile, I called the Ralph's market at 101 G Street, San Diego, and spoke with the managers, Dennis Murphy and Sherry Knoerr. I have ordered for you and your family the biggest Thanksgiving turkey they have. I know you can afford it, but I wanted to do something for you and your family, especially for Thanksgiving. Just stop by Ralph's and ask either Dennis or Sherry for the largest fresh or frozen turkey (on or after November 20, 1999, a Saturday) that they have.

I'm looking forward to seeing you in Denver on January 2, 2000, your last regular season game for the Chargers. How many decades is that for you, Sid? I'm going to miss you. The Chargers will miss you, and the NFL will miss you.

> *Thanks!*
> *Love,*
> *Chris Myrtle*

> *P.S. Dennis and Sherry are expecting you.*

I reached the end of the letter overcome with pride in my ability to invite revenge after so many years. Chip had been waiting all those years to get back at me. I wrote Chip back after my wife and I had finally finished laughing:

> *Dear Chip,*

> *Thank you for the holiday note and well wishes, but you're still the biggest turkey. I'm too old of a cat to be screwed by a kitten.*

> *Sid Brooks*

Faking the Fans

Ed White, a 275-pound, Pro-Bowl offensive lineman nicknamed "Big Ed," was an easy target for pranks. He was jovial and a good sport when it came to the pranks that were pulled on him. Take, for instance, the time the equipment department teased him by writing "WIDE LOAD" on the back of his practice pants in non-erasable ink. I admit we picked on Ed, but it was always with affection.

Ed had been playing football for about 20 years, and Coach Coryell allowed him to take days off from practice to preserve him for game days—but he couldn't tell anybody that. The practice paid off huge dividends, because come Sunday afternoons, Ed was a wide load for the other team to deal with. But one day at training camp, Ed actually missed practice for a legitimate reason: he became ill and was confined to his dorm room. What happened in his absence was quite a memory for at least one person, I'm sure.

There was a fan who showed up each day of training camp that year and watched every practice. The man had the same well-fed build as Ed, and one of the players saw the man leaning on the fence and teased Ed that his brother was waiting for him. The day Ed was laid up, the offensive linemen went out to the practice field before the rest of the team as usual. On the way out someone asked where Ed was, and one of the trainers said Ed wouldn't be practicing that day

Dennis McKnight pointed to the round-bodied gent who had come to watch practice, and said, unable to keep the hilarity from his voice, "What do you mean? There's Ed standing by the fence." His fellow linemen, noting the man's size and shape, laughed along with him.

The spectator was built so much like Ed that an idea popped in my head. Not that I didn't have enough to do during training camp. I was as busy as a flea-infested dog trying to keep himself scratched, but fun occasionally had to trump work. I asked the young man if he would do me a favor and dress in Ed's uniform and go out to field and meet the offensive linemen. He grinned as if he'd been made mascot for the Playboy Club. We took him into the locker room, dressed him in Ed's uniform and sent him out to join the offensive linemen. When the rest of the team went out for warmups they had a big laugh, slapped the guy on the back, and congratulated him for making the team. The Ed White imposter began to believe he belonged out there, hunching his shoulders, getting down in position, and springing forward. I had to come up with a way to get him out of Ed's uniform before he tried to tackle somebody. "Okay," I said. "Go back to the locker room and change into your clothes now. Get out of that uniform."

He said goodbye to the players and jogged, very jock-like, shoulders back, high-stepping back toward the lockers. On his way off the field other fans in the bleachers began waving and yelling, "Ed, Ed." He glanced around at the team preparing for practice behind him. The joke now over and, assuming we'd forgotten about him, he began to play the role of football star. He walked over to the stands and began shaking hands and signing autographs for the crowd before we could usher him back into the locker room and out of Ed's uniform. I don't know how many people think they have Ed White's autograph and don't. That one is on the fans.

How to Stop a Little Big Man

Hank Bauer, one of the best special team players the Chargers ever had, rode a Moped to work during training camp. He talked a bunch of double-do for a short guy in cleats on a small bike. He irritated the other players with his "I'm tougher than you" talk. Everyone predicted he was destined to become a politician or a sports announcer, because he always had an opinion about everything, and felt obliged to share it. Hank told Pat Curran he was too slow to play tight end. Pat was a member of the prankster committee, and decided to show Hank that it wasn't wise to mess with a prankster. "We'll see how fast you are," Pat promised Hank.

There was a wooded area next to our camp offices, where the trees were tall and dense. Hank's little Moped found its way ten feet up a tree, hidden by branches and secured to the tree with yards and yards of adhesive tape. Being low to the Earth's surface compared to some of the other players, Hank hunted and hunted for his bike and didn't think to look up. He searched until dark before he found it. That incident kept Hank quiet for about a second.

Scale Busters

The Chargers had an old Toledo scale in the weight room that the defensive line coaches used to weigh the linemen on every Thursday. Judging by the size of the players who make up the offensive and defensive lines on Sunday, it may not come as a surprise that some of the linemen may have had a slight weight problem.

Coaches and trainers quoted the players a desirable weight for each of them at the beginning of the season. Each player was expected to maintain his goal weight throughout the season or face a fine of a certain dollar amount for each pound gained. To battle the tax, the players—many of them donut addicts, candy bar junkies, and fried chicken carnivores—developed schemes to balance the scales in their favor. Louie Kelcher was their leader. He figured out that if he slid a pack of matches under the front of the scale a certain way he could set the scale so that it registered less than his actual weight. It turned out to work beautifully for a long time. The trick had but one drawback: No one could get on the scale and get an accurate reading after it was set without taking the match pack out. The big guys would weigh in and leave the room. Anyone who hopped on the scales after them was in for a big surprise—sometimes pleasing, sometimes jolting.

One day a rookie defensive back stepped on the scale following the cheaters. He immediately assumed that only a fatal disease could make him lose 20 pounds overnight and sought the advice of the trainers. These trainers had been around for a long time and had seen most of the tricks. After a few minutes of examining the scale, they discovered the problem. The next year all players weighed in on a digital scale. By now, I'm sure that some clever, overweight lineman has, no doubt, figured out a way to de-digitalize the scale.

Under Arrest

Eric Sievers, a tight end drafted in 1981, resided with his grandfather in San Diego during his rookie year. He was close to his grandfather and protective of him, but he hadn't considered his grandfather the night he made fun of Big Ed White. Ed put the pressure on Eric to get up and sing one night in the dining hall, a right of passage for all rookies. Being a rookie, Eric didn't understand that he was in no position to make fun of a veteran. Eric stood and began to sing, "Big Ed White, why are you so big? Could it be because you eat pizza sandwiches?"

That night, after Eric had sung about Ed, the committee went to work. I called some of our friends at the police department and asked if they'd help us put a cocky rookie in his place. The next day at training camp Eric strutted around Ed as if he'd won a boxing match, but Ed chilled, saying nothing. Eric came into the locker room after practice and took a shower, whistling the Big Ed song as the water splashed around him. But it was no laughing matter when the police stormed the locker room and surrounded Eric as he stepped out of the shower before he had even had the chance to dry off. They showed him a wanted poster of him and said, "You're under arrest for suspicion of murder, bank robbery, stealing cars, child abduction, and for being armed and dangerous." Within minutes the cuffs clinked around his wrist while the police read Eric his rights.

"I'm naked," Eric pleaded, looking for someone to come to his aid. There were 107 men in camp, but not one of them offered a word. I slipped between the policemen and wrapped a towel around Eric before the police placed him in the back seat of the squad car. The officers started the car and began to drive off slowly, allowing the large audience of players to witness Eric being driven away.

I banged on the car window, yelling, "Who can I call?" Eric hung his head. He wasn't about to tell me to call his grandfather and subject the old man to such shame. The police car cruised as if in a funeral procession, which added to Eric's misery. Everyone stared.

When the car pulled around the corner from the locker rooms, Ed White stood in the street. The police stopped the car and left Eric on the street in front of Ed White.

"Don't f--k with me ever again, rookie," Ed said, hardly containing his laughter.

Eric sung his school song that night without being asked.

Mistaken Identity

One evening, a few days after Eric Sievers' so-called arrest, about a dozen rookies went to a local pub called The Elephant Bar to relax together. Not long after the players went in and ordered drinks, a couple of policemen came in together and approached running back Clarence Williams. "Step outside with us," the officers said to Clarence.

Clarence turned his back on the policemen and laughed. "They're f--king with us again," he said to his teammates.

"I told you to step outside," the policeman said, this time with authority while placing his hand on his gun. Laughter faded. The clink of glasses fell silent. The others looked to one another with troubled faces. Clarence recognized the seriousness in the officers' commands and, realizing that this was no prank, let the policemen lead him outside.

"You fit the description of someone who robbed a bank this afternoon," the policeman said. "African-American, about your height and weight, and seen in this area."

"That couldn't have been me," Clarence said. "I'm with the Chargers." He began to sweat and looked around for someone to vouch for him. "Go inside and ask the other players. Check with the Chargers' coaches. They'll tell you I've been at practice all day."

Clarence was cleared, of course. And we didn't play any more tricks involving police arrest after that.

Psychological War Is Hell

Certain people in the Chargers' organization thought they could criticize the way I took care of them and get away with it. Toward the end of one training camp, the scouts came by my office and thanked me for keeping them dressed so well. Dwight Adams, Bob Sneddon, Ron Nay, and Ray Newman complimented me on the organization of their Chargers gear, and said how pleased they were with the way the equipment department had taken care of them.

Then fellow scout Red Phillips lambasted me, tongue in cheek: "Would you do something about the way my clothes fit me when I come back next year?" I pointed my finger at him. "Don't mess with me," I said with a smirk. We laughed, and the scouts left.

Next year when Red came in to training camp, I warned the other scouts that I had a surprise for Red so that they'd be there to watch his reaction. A joke played on anyone was only good if there were witnesses. I filled Red's room with old stained pants, used T-shirts, musty towels and washcloths, and scattered beer cans about the room. The other scouts waited outside for Red to go inside and see his room. "Sid got us some good gear this year," Ron Nay said. "Check it out."

Red went in and came right back out. That can't be my room. Someone else must be assigned to this room. All the scouts went in to get a load of Red's home away from home. Ron, one of the world's biggest kidders, said, "I'll get the list with the room assignments." He went to his room and came back with the list. "No, it says right here this is the room assigned to you." They patted Red on his back and lowered their eyes with sympathy. "Why don't you come and see what's in our rooms?"

One by one by one they showed him their rooms. Each of the other rooms was clean and neat. New clothing—shirts, pants, socks, shoes, and other essentials—had been arranged in perfect order.

"I'm going to see about this," Red said.

"We'd better get to our meeting now," Ron replied. "Take care of it when we get back."

While they were in the meeting we removed the junk, and replaced it with all of his actual clothing, filed away neatly. The only alteration—we gave him size 48 pants, a few sizes too large. We hung a sign outside his door with "Red Phillips" written on it, and attached a Polaroid of the junky room to the mirror in his room. When he went to put on his pants, he found a note pinned to them that read, "Don't f--k with any of the committee members." He called the other scouts to share in the joke: "That damned Sid got me again."

Later in the dining room, grinning, he said, "You really got me this time, Sid."

"Psychological war is hell, Red," I replied.

An Eye for An Eye

Junior Seau was the Chargers' No. 1 draft pick in the 1990 NFL draft, and the No. 5 pick overall. The players drooled over the hefty size of Junior's signing bonus and teased him about being "Mr. Moneyman." During our first road trip that year most of the players stayed in their rooms for the evening meal on Saturday night. Usually they went out to eat, but no one paid much attention to their decision to stay in, chalking it up to early season jitters. That night bed check was a breeze. Sunday morning the team members were required to check out of the hotel and pay for any incidentals occurred to their rooms before boarding the bus for the game. When Junior went to check out, the cashier handed him a bill for $2,800.

"Can you check that again?" Junior said. "There has to be some mistake."

"There's no mistake. You had fifty meals and soft drinks signed to your room. Somebody ate well last night. The bill is correct."

Junior shook his head back and forth. "They got me."

"What do you mean they got you?" asked the cashier. "Who are *they*?"

"My teammates had dinner on me. They want to play; the game is on. I will get one of those vets."

A month went by, and Junior didn't mention the dinners. He called a friend of his who owned a florist and ordered three floral arrangements for all the females in the Chargers organization—sixteen in all—to be delivered on Tuesday, the players' day off. Gary Plummer came in on Wednesday, and, as he did every Wednesday, went upstairs to meet with the defensive coaches. As he went down the hall, one after the other, the ladies ran up to him and thanked him for the roses and told him how nice it was of him to send them all flowers. Gary acknowledged their thanks and didn't let on that he was in the dark about where the flowers came from. He wondered how the credit went to him for the gesture, but he didn't say anything about it to anyone. A few days later the bill from the florist arrived in the locker room for him. Gary laughed.

"Damn you, Seau," he said, "I know it was you. Don't forget you're still a rookie, and I can bend you like a piece of weak wire."

The room exploded with laughter.

Finding His Voice

Defensive back Rodney Harrison's refusal to sing at the dinner table was a big rookie mistake. Rubin Davis demanded to hear Rodney's pipes, but Rodney the tough guy responded, "I won't sing, and you can't make me."

"Oh yeah? Wait and see," Rubin responded. But nothing else was said to Rodney about singing, so he walked around like a proud young cock, smug about his bravado. He was too new to understand that a rookie never won these battles.

Later on in the preseason the Chargers were playing a game in Berlin, Germany. Our hotel has nearly 30 stories tall, which gave the veterans an idea. Some very large members of the team—including Rubin, Courtney Hall, Chris Mimms, Harry Swyane, and Leslie O'Neal—waited until Rodney had retired to his room for the evening. Then this big band of heavies went to

Rodney's room and knocked on his door. Rodney opened the door and his teammates grabbed him, pinned him down, and stripped him bare. They used adhesive tape to bind his feet and hands, and then they placed him on the elevator and pushed the buttons to each and every floor, from the top to the bottom.

Nice guys John Carney and John Kidd felt sorry for him and rescued Rodney from complete humiliation. But the rookie suffered tape burns from the adhesive, and was forced to swallow his pride. Back at camp, without being asked, he sang like a bird that was just happy to be able to fly.

11

THE BOLT RECIPE

The Secret of Hang Time

I f you've ever wondered in amazement at the flight of the ball that a punter sends sailing high above the field, seemingly hanging in the air longer than a helium-filled balloon at the fair, then here's a little secret about hang time never before revealed to the public. But let me first say that I have never been a conspirator in NFL sabotage. I plead the fifth to any wrongdoing, but I have always been on the side of the players on the Chargers' team. I helped them with whatever they needed in order to win the trophy, and when necessary, I was blind.

Wilson Sporting Goods provided the official footballs used by NFL teams along with appropriate directions for preparing balls for game day. Each team is allotted 360 balls per season. Before each game at home, the home team equipment manager prepares 24 footballs for the game. The NFL rule states that all game balls must be prepared properly and consistently inflated with exactly 13 pounds of air. The rule strictly prohibits any person from altering the fundamental structure, defacing, or reshaping the surface characteristics of a football to be used in a game. If any individual alters the game balls, or if a in appropriate ball is used in a game, the person responsible is subject to a $25,000 fine.

Until the late '90s, a representative from the equipment department delivered these footballs to the officials' locker room two hours and 15 minutes before game time, at which point the referees checked the balls for final approval. Of all the football players, only the quarterback was allowed to handle the balls officially used in the game by briefly passing them during pregame warmups. If one ball did not meet the quarterback's satisfaction, then another ball was issued. So the rest of the team could only warm up with balls that had been used during regular practice—not game balls.

Rules are made to be broken, boys will be boys, and your grandmother's dose of turpentine and sugar proved good for something other than a stomachache. In a covert operation in the back room, kickers applied turpentine on the balls and rubbed off the new texture. The point of doing so was to improve the ball's hang time. Whether or not the turpentine worked is debatable, but the fact remains that at this time kickers and punters were kicking the ball higher than at any time before in NFL history.

The NFL became aware that something was being done to the balls without knowing what or how. NFL headquarters sent memos to the equipment managers with the correct preparations for the game balls, and directed Wilson to send the balls directly to the equipment managers in sealed boxes to prevent anyone from tampering with the balls, and with a renewed warning to fine anyone who altered a ball. The punter, kicker, and some equipment managers unsealed the boxes with extreme care, worked the footballs over, the sealed the boxes as though they hadn't been touched.

The application process was called the "Bolt Recipe," which follows in code:

- Firmly wipe down potato (football) with very damp/wet brush (towel). Do not worry if potato gets too wet.
- Place five potatoes in a potato sack (cotton laundry bag). Do not use mesh bag; this will rub off the dimples on the potato.
- Dry in industrial oven (clothes dryer) for ten minutes on medium-high heat. If potato comes out really burnt, reduce heat. Take about five pounds of air out of the potato and work the seams and points with hands and knees. A good position to do this is to kneel on a couple of towels and lean over to press the potato against the floor. Place a towel on the floor under the potato.
- Using silverware (ball pump), pump up potato with approximately 20 pounds of air and leave overnight.
- In the morning bring potato back to 13 pounds of air. Brush with Wilson brush until tacky. Do not brush too much. If the potato becomes too shiny, you brushed too much.
- Now the potato is ready for the market.

Recipe for Disaster

One day Scott Kaplin, a rookie kicker, was assigned to cook the potatoes. The veteran kickers sent him to the kitchen (laundry room) to place the potatoes in the oven (dryer) for ten minutes. Scott didn't have a clue about cooking potatoes, but rookies knew better than to question veterans. After 15 minutes of keeping watch, John Kidd, the kicker, stuck his head inside a slant opening in the kitchen door and whispered, "What are you doing in there so long? It only takes ten minutes."

"I can't get the door open," Scott replied.

"Can't get what door open?"

"Dryer."

"What kind of football player can't open the door to a dryer?" John wondered aloud.

John went in the laundry room to check out the problem and discovered Scott trying to open the door to the washing machine. The washing machines operated on pre-set cycles. Once the cycle started, the machine did not respond to Scott's feeble attempts to intercept its run, and the washer splashed and churned on to complete its mission. The room was like a sauna. Hot air from the dryers swamped the cramped space. Sweat trickled down Scott's face. His eyes, wide with fear and frustration, darted back and forth from the washer to the locker room. Scott's problem was simple: he couldn't differentiate a washing machine from a dryer, and so on that day the potatoes were drowned.

Still Flying High

There were spies watching spies in the NFL. Somehow the league discovered that the balls were being altered, but still the Bolt Recipe remained a mystery. This time, NFL headquarters instructed Wilson to send the balls, thoroughly prepared and conditioned, directly to the officiating crew at the hotel the day before the game. The referees tested the balls in their locker room, divided them in two sets of 12, and placed them in two Wilson bags. Before the game the officials went over how to get the balls on and off the field with the ball boys. The referees took one bag of balls out at the beginning of the game. The 12 remaining balls were secured in the officials' locker room.

The league probably felt certain they had succeeded in putting a hitch in the special team's git-a-long, but determination outsmarted defeat. I hired Rocky Baham, the officials' locker room attendant, to become one of my undercover agents. He was a diehard Chargers fan, and somehow on his watch six of the officials' balls were switched with bolt recipe balls before half time. When the 12 remaining balls landed on the field before the second half, six were cooked potatoes. Three ball boys stationed on each side of the field knew to throw the doctored balls in for the kickers. Catch me if you can, the saying goes.

After I retired from the Chargers, the NFL came up with a new system for controlling the kicking balls. The balls are specifically marked, "kicking balls." Ball boys handling kicking balls must wear a big red X on their uniforms. But even with the precautions, balls are still flying high. Perhaps it never was the balls, but the kickers who made the balls soar. Or maybe the kickers have cooked up another recipe? Possibly that story has yet to be told.

12

HEAD COACH

A Costly Speech

In my 27 years with the Chargers, I worked with ten head coaches, and I would welcome the opportunity to work with each of them again. Some of the working relationships were brief, because a few didn't stay long, but most have remained life-long friends. Many assistant coaches—Ernie Zampese, Bill Walsh, Joe Gibbs, Jim Hanifan, Willie Wood, Dick Corey, Ted Tollner, and Dave Levy—and many others touched my life in a special way. All of them were respectful and accepted me into the NFL football family.

Although he was not a head coach with the Chargers, I would be remiss if I didn't talk about Gibbs, then the offensive coordinator for San Diego. Gibbs was present when coach Don Coryell allowed me to give a pregame speech. That happened during a playoff game against the Houston Oilers in 1979.

The Oilers were banged up. Quarterback Dan Pastorini, running back Earl Campbell, and fullback Rob Carpenter were all injured. With three of Houston's best players out, and the Chargers in top form, we were a shoo-in to win. Coryell called the team together, addressed them with his pregame speech, and then said, "I've got a guy here who has something to say. Go ahead, Sid."

I moved to the center of the room, clenched my fists, and raised them into the air. "Go out there and beat them like Sherman did when he walked through Georgia," I said. "I wish I could play them." I picked up a pair of cleats and threw them against the wall. "Let's go out and kick their butts up one side and down the other." I had always wanted the opportunity to say that, thinking that was the way to really fire a team up. And it sure worked: Guys began pushing and shoving, trying to get through the door in pairs to get out to the field.

I fired them up all right. We lost the game (17-14), the chance to go on to the Super Bowl, and the opportunity to earn a lot of playoff money. And Gibbs jokingly blamed my speech for the team's loss.

He won't let me forget it, either. Years later, I ran into Joe Gibbs at the airport in Washington, D.C. "Stop that man," he yelled. "He owes me $35,000 dollars."

Coach Coryell

Coach Coryell, who was at the helm of the Chargers from 1978-86, was the ultimate players coach. He loved the game of football, and he loved his players. He made his players feel like they mattered, always encouraging and reassuring them. Offensive lineman Dennis McKnight once told me that when he tried out for the Chargers he had already been through three teams' camps, and was cut each time. McKnight had his doubts about making the team, and spent every day a nervous wreck. At the end of a practice Coryell came up to McKnight and put his arm around him. "I just love you. I love your spirit," Coryell said. "You're going to make it in this league."

Coryell's players believed in him, because he believed in them. If Coryell told them to jump through a window, they'd run as hard as they could and jump through the window, no questions asked. That's the sort of relationship he had with his players.

Time meant nothing to Coryell as long as he spent it preparing for the game. Under his watch, the number of minicamps increased and preseason began earlier. I learned not to expect much of an off-season. With him, the football season lasted all year. He drove himself hard, and expected the same from everyone around him.

Coryell's enthusiasm brought the glory days to the Chargers. There was a feeling of power on the team and in the city of San Diego with Coryell in charge. "Air Coryell," as we called him on occasion, and his field officers—Bill Walsh, Jim Hanifan, Joe Gibbs, Ted Tollner, Ernie Zampese, and Dave Levy—led the league in offense four times during his stint with the Chargers. Stacked with talent, his defense was probably as good as it gets in football, but Coryell liked to score points. He was happiest when the ball soared, thus the name, "Air Coryell."

Killer Instincts

Coach Coryell liked to rouse his players by depicting them as killer bees or killer dogs. One game in Seattle he referred to Steve Largent as the bunny the killer dogs had to catch. Before the game, Ed White was in the bathroom trying to fit all of himself into his uniform when he spotted coach Coryell in the mirror behind him. Coryell loved Ed, his talent, and his durability. Ed had played in the league quite a few years, having come to the Chargers from the Vikings.

"Ed, you got to do me a favor," Coryell said.

"What is it, Coach?" Ed asked. "I'm trying to get ready here."

"We've got to be killer dogs. I need you to bark like a dog and get the fellows fired up."

"Coach, I can't bark," Ed replied.

"You have to do it, Ed. You can't let me down," pleaded Coryell. "We got to get that bunny!"

In the meeting with the rest of the team, Coryell bent over from the waist, hands on his knees with his head pointed in a hunting dog position, said, "Today, fellows, we've got to be killer dogs!" He then looked over at Ed, waiting for him to bark. But Ed, not into his performance at all, merely uttered a weak, "Woof, woof."

"God dang it, Ed," Coryell said, uttering his favorite swear word as he stood up straight and turned red in the face. "That's no killer dog." He appeared ready to smack Ed.

By now, everyone else was ready to crack up. Without any prompting, Jessie Penrose rose from his seat and began growling and barking so dog-like, that by his lonesome he sounded like a pack of mad dogs. Coryell's face broke into a grin. He gave Jessie a big hug and shouted, "Lets go get 'em."

If I remember correctly, the Chargers lost that game, and Coryell cut Jessie right after the game. Ed White remained because he had what Coryell wanted in his players—a killer instinct—even if he wasn't willing to bark like a dog to prove it.

Back Against the Wall

The Chargers faced a big game in Denver. If San Diego lost, they'd be out of the playoffs. Coryell, in his attempt to demonstrate just how critical the game was, stood in front of a chair centered at the halfway point of a 50-foot long room. He had belted his pants up so high that his socks were showing. Every man on the team was a fashion critic, and no one was exempt when it came to poking fun. The players began snickering under their breath as soon as Coach walked, and it only got worse throughout the meeting.

When he opened his mouth to address the team, he began backing up toward the far end of the wall. "Gosh darn, fellows, they got us backed up against a wall," Coryell said over and over. Each time he said it he backed farther away. Pretty soon he had literally backed up against the far wall—so far from the team they could hardly hear him any longer. Most were holding their sides to keep from laughing out loud. Bob Klein recorded the whole thing on tape, and when the meeting ended they went up to their hotel rooms, played the tape, and laughed some more.

Ed White and Don Macek went downstairs to the lobby to take a bathroom break. They were sitting in side-by-side stalls. Ed said, "Donnie, did you see Coach back up until he was out of sight? Can you believe him, man? That was so damned funny. And did you see how high those pants were hiked up, man? I bit a hole in my lip to keep from losing it. I almost wet my pants."

They'd talked about him and laughed for a couple minutes when all of a sudden a pair of black, wing-tip shoes appeared on the floor in front of Ed's stall, followed by a sliver of a face that could be seen through the crack of the door.

"Ed," Coryell said in that clipped voice of his that everyone loved. "Be careful who you talk about so anyone might hear. You never know who you're sitting next to."

Left Behind

We played the Raiders in Los Angeles during their separation from Oakland. It was a two-hour bus trip from San Diego to the Coliseum where the Raiders had taken up residence. Pat Curran, tight end turned business manager for the Chargers, arranged our transportation, and loaded the team onto three buses. Trucks transported the equipment behind us.

After each game, Pat routinely checked the locker room for stray players before leaving for San Diego. This time, as usual he went through the locker room, yelling loud enough to wake everyone from Los Angeles to San Juan Capistrano, "Is everybody out?" Getting no answer, and assuming everyone was aboard the bus, he gave the bus drivers the go ahead. Off we headed for San Diego down the 5 Freeway. Pat rode on bus number three. About halfway to Santa Ana Pat noted that Coach Coryell was not on board, and asked if anyone had seen him. No one answered.

Pat checked, and he wasn't on the first bus. The driver radioed bus number two and asked if Coryell was on his bus, and again the answer was no. In a panic, Pat informed the driver that we had to turn around at the next exit and hurry back to the Coliseum. At the exit, Pat spotted a 7-Eleven convenience store and asked the driver to stop. He got off the bus, got back on with a case of beer, deposited a six-pack on the seat next to him, and passed the rest out to the players on board.

"I'm not facing this one sober," he said. "And I had better have a peace offering with me when I get there."

When we reached the tunnel at the Coliseum, the driver drove around for a while before we spied Al Davis, the Raiders' owner, Don Coryell, and Don's two escorts standing beside Al's limousine.

Al Davis had offered to drive Coach Coryell back to San Diego, "But I'm not taking your two goons," he was reported to have said about Don's escorts.

Coryell had suspected Al Davis of spying on his team practices, and not trusting him fully, he didn't know if Mr. Davis' offer was legitimate. So he declined his offer and was waiting around bewildered in the parking lot when our bus pulled up. Coryell got on the bus and sat down next to Pat. Nobody said a word all the way back to San Diego, but every can of beer, including the six-pack on Don's seat, was empty by the time we arrived back home. You could tell by the dejection on his face that he was hurt and disappointed, more than angry.

The bus pulled into the San Diego stadium parking lot, and the players on the second bus waited to see if the coach had been found. The air was charged with hilarity, but no one dared to laugh. Coryell got in his car and left, and the players filed out of the bus, picked up their cars and went home. The next day after a very quiet morning meeting, someone said, "Has anyone seen Pat Curran?," and the house erupted in laughter.

That was the one and only time a Chargers coach was left behind.

Lose the Yellow Jackets

Every week I contacted Starter, our clothing provider, and surprised the coaching staff, who loved receiving new clothing, with a new addition to their wardrobe. For a game against Pittsburgh in 1984, I purchased new jackets in the Chargers gold for the coaches to wear on the sideline. In that game, Charlie Joiner set a NFL record with his 650th pass reception in the fourth quarter.

The game didn't go well for the Chargers in the beginning. James Brooks, a speedster and top-notch return man, fumbled the opening kickoff in Pittsburgh territory. The Steelers picked up the ball and scored. Again with James Brooks set to receive, Pittsburgh kicked the ball and it slid through Brooks' hands again. Pittsburgh picked up the ball and took it over the goal line a second time. The score was 14-0 after 30 seconds of play. Coryell's face turned purple. He strutted on the sideline like a rooster getting ready for a cock fight.

Brooks, who was not prone to fumble and was disheartened after his disappointing performance, went to the sideline to get some additional tacky (a sticky substance used to improve catching ability) for his gloves. Coach Coryell's son had come along on the trip and prior to the game, he attempted to assist Brooks without Brooks' knowledge. Instead of coating his gloves with tacky, he lathered them up in Vaseline. When I learned of this, I made certain that Coryell didn't catch word of it. When James came to me, I switched his gloves and fixed his problem.

The closest Coach Coryell had ever come to cursing was when he yelled, "Gosh darn!" But at halftime, still fuming and unaware of the misunderstanding that had caused his first-half disaster, he came into the locker room and shouted, "Get them God damned yellow jackets out of here! I don't want to see them again."

Fortunately for me, the jackets were reversible. I had the coaches turn the coats inside out to the blue side for the duration of the game, and wouldn't you know it, the Chargers won. We never wore those jackets on their yellow side again.

Al Saunders

Al Saunders took over as head coach midway through the 1986 season. He was younger and much more taken with his position than Coryell. He dressed with pride as a professional on game day and even in practice. We had enjoyed a good relationship while he served as an assistant head coach under Coryell, so his authoritative behavior upon his promotion surprised me. But I understood the pressure that came along with his new job. Al remained friendly with me, but standoffish.

His first year, as no head coach had done before, he excluded the dungeon crew from the team picture, which threw us a bit. But every morning before practice he stopped in the locker room and asked, in an administrative way, "How is everything down here?"

I respected the man's agenda and individuality. The following year, after the newness of Al's position wore off, we were back in the team picture. But Al only lasted two full seasons.

Dan Henning and the Missing Seat

Dan Henning came on board as head coach in 1989 and quickly became one of the boys. Like all the other coaches I had the privilege to work with, he vowed to win, and he wanted a smooth-sailing ship. Monday afternoon after a game, he came down to my office in the locker room and brought the week's schedule. I kept it on my chalk board with the month's activities. Our trainer, Keoki Kamau, Coach Henning, and I went over the schedule together.

Henning was generous, sharing with his staff and the dungeon crew his contract with Starter. He passed the catalog around, allowing us to order what we wanted for ourselves and our families. In another venture, Slim Fast provided him with a new wardrobe of his choosing after he signed a contract with them to advertise his weight-loss using their program. He could select whatever he wanted to wear from a clothing company in New York, and Slim Fast footed the bill.

I represented the Chargers at the NFL draft in New York every April. While the pickings were still good, Dan sent me to choose any clothing item I wanted from his Slim Fast account. At that year's draft, he made sure I was well suited. Henning dressed his staff, took us to dinner, and made sure we enjoyed our staff meetings.

There was no reason not to believe that the dungeon crew would fail to come to his defense when the fans attacked him for not winning. No attack on any coach had ever been so mean-spirited as in the case of the fan who declared that he wouldn't sit in his seat at the games until Dan Henning had been removed as head coach. Henning was a friend to the dungeon crew, and even though we all knew the name of the game of football was winning, we liked having him around.

After that fan's announcement came out in the newspaper, I came into the locker room before the next home game and was greeted by Keoki. "Come here," he said. "I want to show you something."

I followed him to the training room where he opened a closet door and showed me a big cardboard box.

"Take a look inside," Keoki said, laughing uncontrollably.

I lifted the lid of the box. Inside sat the seat of the of the disgruntled season ticket holder. I knew the seat by the number that had appeared in the newspaper article. My eyebrows went up. "How did that get in here?" I asked.

"Well," Keoki said, "he's not going to sit in it again until Henning is fired, so it was just sitting there taking up space. Someone made it easy for that guy not to change his mind."

Hours later we went out for pregame warmups. I looked up in the stands, and the empty space where the seat had been stood out like a missing tooth among the rows of seats. Spectators had begun to file in, but the row with the missing seats remained empty. When we came back out for the game, a man and a woman stood in the seat space surrounded by several stadium security guards, and a crowd had gathered around them. Keoki and I could hardly control our laughter.

On Monday following that game, the *Union-Tribune* ran the story of the missing seat, and speculated on who had removed it. Henning was amused by the whole affair, but that act of retaliation didn't save his job. Rumors are still out there about the guilty culprits.

Coach "Boss" Bobby Ross

Bobby Ross, who took over in 1992 and was head coach through the 1996 season, was a caring, a Southern gentleman with high expectations for his staff and players. He wasn't afraid of the administration, but was considerate of the equipment and training staff, allowing us to carry out our duties in our usual manner. Bobby Ross was generally composed, but when he barked, he did it like a drill sergeant and carried out his responsibilities with military discipline. I hardly ever saw him riled, except one Sunday when we went to Los Angeles to play the Raiders.

The Chargers played the Raiders twice each year, at home and at the Coliseum. On one occasion at the Raiders' house, someone from LA had brought a TV out into the hallway outside our locker room before the game, and their players hung around drinking coffee, watching the other games before our game began, and talking loudly. This TV watching and coffee drinking by the Raiders irritated Bobby, because it became a distraction for his players. The Chargers' players had to squeeze and push past them to get out of our locker room, sometimes stopping to watch the game on TV. Bobby Ross steamed.

"Do what you have to do," Bobby told Keoki and me before our next trip up to play the Raiders. "Get rid of that television before I see it again. I don't care how you do it. If it's playing when I get there, I'm going to throw a brick through it."

We hadn't seen that side of Bobby Ross yet. This was a kind man who held gatherings at his home for the whole team, a man who handled adversity with diplomacy and who prayed before every game for the players' safety. But we knew he was serious about his threat. So Keoki and I went up the night before the game, making sure we were there at a time when there were no witnesses.

The Raiders kept the despised TV locked in the club office. Keoki told the guard at the Coliseum that the Chargers were about to make a trade, and he needed to use the office to make a confidential phone call about the medical status of the player in the trade. I guarded the door by moving trunks in front of it. Keoki spoke behind the closed doors as if he were carrying on a conversation with someone, but he was actually busy cutting wires on the TV, hoping he'd severed the ones that would put the TV out of service.

On Sunday morning we spied on the Raiders as they tried to get their TV to work. The thing was as dead as a junked car with no batteries. Bobby Ross smiled knowingly. Later, they replaced the disabled TV with a small black and white. Someone in our locker joked that they had sent one of their people out to buy a replacement.

For Bobby Ross, we would have and should have cut the cable.

Kevin Gilbride

Kevin Gilbride, whose tenure lasted just a season and a half, was very businesslike, but could be highly explosive when provoked. He was most always considerate of the locker-room staff, and respected our way of making sure his team was taken care off. He demanded accountability and responsibility from his players. He didn't stay in San Diego long enough for us to figure out the right prank to play on him, but I got to know Kevin well enough to appreciate the fact that he would have loved it.

June Jones

Mr. Laid-Back, June Jones knew he was only going to be with the Chargers for a few months when he took over after Gilbride left. But despite his short stay, he knew the game of football. June had the football knowledge to turn the team around, but I don't think he considered staying with the Chargers as the right choice for him, which didn't matter because he wasn't given much of a chance.

An affable guy, June was our man down in the basement. "Whatever you've been doing has worked so far," he told Keoki and me. "However you want to run the schedule is okay with me. I trust you guys to know what you're doing."

Keoki and I wrote every itinerary, while June concentrated on the game. It was a love-love relationship that ended too soon.

Mike Riley

After Bobby Ross left, the door of the Chargers' head coach's office opened and closed so often that I had to read the roster to learn who'd be leading the team that week. Mike Riley came in to his first NFL head-coaching job in 1999 with a boyish look, but he carried himself like a seasoned coach among the old pros, dedicated to his work and his philosophy. During the one year I worked with him, I watched him try to make the players believe in his program and work within it.

I said goodbye to Mike Riley at the end of his first season when I retired in 2000.

13

Everything You Wanted to Know about Football Players, but were Afraid to Ask

First, the Really Good Stuff

Besides being playful, funny, gullible, and superstitious, the football players I know are sensitive, generous humanitarians. They like to have fun, drive expensive cars, and play their music loud, but these football players are also men who have heart. Our special care of them in the locker room paid off. When the time came to transport that pampered feeling out of the locker room and into the community, every player I asked to participate in a charity event said yes. Throughout my 27 years, I witnessed players giving—not just monetary contributions, but their time and effort—to charitable events and individual causes.

While their contributions on the field brought them far greater praise, their efforts off the field should not go without notice. These players worked hard to help make our community a better place.

For the Love of Children

The beneficiaries of the players' fundraisers were often children. Terrell Fletcher held Toss for Tots to fund research to find a cure for asthma. Rodney Harrison hosted Hard Hitter to improve literacy for underprivileged youth. David Binn, John Parrella, Fred McCray, and Aaron Taylor all donated their time for the well being of the Children's Hospital. John Carney's Fresh Start organization was created to raise funds to provide free reconstructive surgery to children with deformities. The Stan Humphries Golf Classic was started to benefit San Diego's Children's Hospital, and to support the Brooke Humphries Fund, named for Stan's daughter. The fund goes toward a children's Home Care Program, which helps children lead a normal life at home rather than being hospitalized.

I was involved in children's charities as well, with a little help from Dan Fouts. My friend, Norma Hirsch, began a campaign to raise money for the prevention of child abuse in San Diego. In 1995 she came to me and asked if I could get some of the Chargers players to help with her cause. Many football players, on the Chargers team and around the league, held golf tournaments to raise money for charitable organizations, but none had put on a bowling tournament. So Dan and I decided on a celebrity bowling event, giving way to the Dan Fouts Celebrity Bowling tournament. Dan spent much of his spare time assuring the success of our venture.

Other Chargers graciously gave their time to the event, including Gill Byrd, Tim Fox, Bill Johnston, Charlie Joiner, Dennis McKnight, and Eric Sievers. And Chargers owner Alex Spanos, upon learning of the event, contributed a sizable donation and agreed to serve as honorary chairman. Celebrities from all areas of entertainment offered to help, including players from other NFL teams, athletes from other sports, actors, and local media celebrities. The first two years, the event raised more than $40,000 for the prevention of child abuse. Back then, that was a lot of money.

By 1987, the number of celebrities donating their time to the effort quadrupled, and the money raised went to help build and furnish the Polinsky Home for severely abused children in San Diego.

A Caring Christmas

In a combined community effort with Norma Hirsch and members of The Child Abuse Prevention Foundation, police chief Bill Kolander and members of the San Diego police department, and 50 members of the San Diego Chargers team, we held a Christmas party for over 200 children in foster care. Each child received a present, was served ice cream and cookies, and got to visit with the players. The foster parents waited in a separate room, so the children would feel free to relax and enjoy themselves.

Chargers defensive back Danny Walters was touched by a little girl whose parents had brutally broken both her legs. She could barely walk, but her smile lit the room. With eyes moist, Danny walked her around the room. The circumstances of some of these kids' lives were difficult to comprehend. Danny didn't want the little girl's happiness to end with a present, ice cream, and cookies. He asked the foster parents if he could take her Christmas shopping the following day, and they agreed to meet the following morning. Danny was so anxious for the trip to begin that he showed up 15 minutes early. A few minutes later the family drove up in a dilapidated car that was putt-putting into the parking lot. They got into Danny's big, black Mercedes Benz and headed to Toys-R-Us.

"Get whatever you want," he told the girl. "I want you to have whatever you want."

Back at the stadium, the little girl climbed back in her family's car, now loaded down with toys. When she rode away with her foster family, her smile once again lit up the world.

Dressing the Part

No Charger player ever turned me down when I asked him to play a part in any charity event involving children. The Chargers' public relations department was aware of my involvement in helping to organize player participation and didn't discourage it. Gil Byrd, Al Saunders, and Eric Sievers volunteered to help the Drug Enforcement Administration with teaching youth drug awareness. Kellen Winslow, Ed White, Donny Macek, and Russ Washington were the original volunteers for police community relations. Wes Chandler braved the challenge of addressing gang members. These players were all aware of the vulnerability of our youth.

Every year, from 1981 to 1986, the whole team visited the kids in the Children's Hospital at Christmas. This was a joint program with the San Diego Police Department. The Greek, a limo service in San Diego, donated a bus to take the players to and from the hospital. Players first visited the children confined to beds, often thrilling the parents much more than the children. Afterwards the hospital furnished cookies and ice cream for the players to pass out to the children in the out-patient department.

While the refreshments were served, the players dressed to entertain the children. One Christmas Drew Gissinger—6 feet, 5 inches, and 279 pounds—donned a Santa Claus suit, and Lionel James—5 feet, 6 inches, and 171 pounds—dressed as an elf. After that visit no one would dress up, because, for the longest time, Lionel caught so much hell from the other players for dressing the part of an elf.

Game Ball

On one visit to the hospital, running back Chuck Muncie bonded with a boy who had two broken legs. The boy had been injured when struck by a car. Chuck had also been hit by a car as a kid and was moved by the boy's circumstances.

"We're going to win the game this weekend for you," Chuck said. "I'm going to see to it."

Some of Chuck's teammates raised their eyebrows and snickered. They knew that Chuck had made promises in the past, but had forgotten about them shortly thereafter. There was a lot of doubt that the kid would ever see Chuck again, but the kid's eyes shone bright with hope, and Chuck seemed reluctant to leave when we said goodbye to the kids.

The Sunday before the game, Chuck called the boy at the hospital. "I'm going to do this game for you," he reiterated. The other players laughed. But when Chuck took the ball on game day, he ran on legs that seemed to fly, scoring two touchdowns. The Chargers won, and on Monday before he showed up for practice, Chuck took the game ball to the hospital and gave it to his new friend. For doing so, Chuck was cheered by his teammates, not just for his deed, but also for simply remembering.

The Junior Seau Foundation, and Others

Established in 1995 to help young people, the largest annual fundraiser is the three-day Junior Seau Celebrity Golf Classic, which attracts celebrities from all walks of life. The fund provides scholarships to financially challenged scholars without the means to pursue their dreams. Junior is also involved in raising money for Shop with a Jock, which benefits underprivileged children. And on Thanksgiving, Seau's The Restaurant serves dinner to 600 residents of homeless shelters, victims of domestic violence, and military families.

For the Love of Critters—the Two- and Four-Legged Kind

Rolf Benirschke, San Diego's beloved kicker and a lover of animals, named his charity "Kicks for Critters." His kicks helped raise money for the San Diego Zoo's Center for Reproduction of Endangered Species. Rolf, a quiet, lovable guy, was a favorite on the team. Everyone was a little overprotective of him, because he'd suffered some health problems that had interrupted his football career for a while. Yet his teammates knew how to find something funny in even the most serious moments. Rolf's teammates supported his "Kicks for Critters" charity, but when his actual kicks landed short or wide of the goalposts, they greeted him in the following day's morning meeting with the sounds of dying animals. His teasing teammates would howl, yelp, and play dead by curling up on the floor. There was a price to pay for being admired.

On the serious side, those football players banded together to help Rolf after his bout with Ulcerative Colitis threatened his life. His teammates organized the largest blood drive in San Diego history, in order to replace his blood loss during his illness. To make it a fun time for the donors, and to encourage people to come out, the Chargers put on a fashion show that featured players and their wives as models. Even I strutted my stuff a few times on the runway. The blood drive has continued every year.

Military Men

I served 20 years in the Air Force. My duties took me to Korea and to Vietnam, an unpopular war. Greeted by protestors who were waving flags and shouting insults, I believed then, as I had before, that being a member of the Armed Forces was something to be proud of. Many of the football players I worked with had no idea of the disciplined training one goes through in the military, or how young some of the troops were. I hoped that by introducing the two groups of young warriors to each other, that through their meeting the soldiers might imbue the athletes with their sense of dedication, professionalism, and teamwork. In turn, I thought the experience might lift the spirits of the troops.

I met the Blue Angels through Captain Larry Pearson, a former Blue Angel, who was stationed at Miramar Marine Corps

Air Station in California. The Blues were kind enough to come out to our practice at training camp, and in turn did a few fly-overs to shake the team up, even taking a few of the bravest players up for a spin. Flying with the Blues was not just for fun, however. It taught the players the importance of paying atten-tion to detail, of alertness, and teamwork.

The same mutual admiration bloomed on the Navy ships we visited, for instance with Vice Admiral Mike Bowman and Vice Admiral Mike McCabe on the USS Kitty Hawk. The sail-ors were impressed with the size and unassuming nature of the football players. In turn, the football players were shocked to discover the responsibilities of 18- and 21-year-old men, and the knowledge they commanded of their duties. The players enjoyed their visit so much that talk about it in the locker room found guys fighting to be the next to go. It was a learning experience for both sides. After flying with the Blue Angels, Terrell Fletcher said the pilots' teamwork, the camaraderie of the members, and their will to get it right for the common goal sounded a lot like what the Chargers were supposed to be doing.

We had such a good relationship with the military that Navy Captain Charles Brady sent me a letter stating that he wanted a picture of the Chargers up in space for his crew. I sent him a T-shirt, which was flown aboard the U.S. space shuttle Columbia. Launch occurred on June 20, 1996, from the Ken-nedy Space Center. The shuttle orbited the earth 271 times at a mean altitude of 153 nautical miles and a speed of 17,500 miles per hour, traveling a total of seven million miles. Dr. Chuck Brady, the shuttle physician, wore the shirt during his space ship exercises aboard the shuttle, putting the Chargers on top of the world.

The Superstitions and Idiosyncrasies

Football players are kind—as you know by this point in the chapter—but they also can be a bit weird, or at least supersti-tious. (Even Donny Macek was superstitious—about being superstitious.) One superstition was that all Chargers players had to shake my hand on the way out to the playing field on game day. Maybe they were only trying to ease tension. Or maybe they were trying to scrape together wisdom from the touch of an old veteran of two wars who had been lucky enough to stay alive through Vietnam. All I know is that I stood in the doorway and slapped hands with each of them before every game.

One day Russ Washington had run out for the game, realized that he had forgotten to shake my hand, and returned to the locker room from the field just to shake my hand. I professed, and still do profess, to being the luckiest man alive. But every player had his own unique rituals that had to be followed. Charlie Joiner would not wear anything new. All his gear had to be battered and worn. If he had anything new, he banged it up before he dressed for a game. Louie Kelcher had to have all brand new, soft clothing before a game. His pregame snack consisted of two Snickers bars, which had to be kept in the back of his locker, where no one else would spot them. Gill Byrd was a fan of chocolate, too. He required two chocolate bars placed strategically in the right side of his locker before a game. But not everyone was a chocolate man. Wilbur Young liked donuts, but wouldn't eat fresh ones. So we hid donuts for him to eat the following day, and nicknamed him "Day Old."

Lockers were a big deal, too. John Carney was only comfortable with the first locker on the end row for all home games. Darren Bennett had to be in the locker next to him. Meanwhile, Dan Fouts was the only player with a big chair in front of his Locker. It was good to be the king. As for cleanliness, Ed White—who required me to place three pieces of gum in his mouth prior to every game—kept the messiest locker. Charlie Joiner kept the neatest locker. His locker was as orderly as a military recruit's.

Of course, I became well acquainted with each player's quirks concerning their equipment. Joe Washington insisted that I bring along 12 pairs of shoes—specifically for him—on every road trip. Hank Bauer was adamant about having two pairs of shoulder pads for every game, at home and away. During the memorable playoff game against Miami during the 1981 season, Kellen Winslow's shoulder pads broke, so I had to use Hank's spare. Hank has never let me hear the last of it to this day.

Speaking of shoulder pads, Russ Washington, Harry Swayne, Monte Hall, Gary Johnson, Louie Kelcher, Donnie Macek, Eric Moton, and Courtney Hall all insisted that I—and no one else—help them into their shoulder pads and jerseys each Sunday. We had a routine without saying a word. If one of them wanted me to adjust the pad on the left shoulder, he would slap that shoulder with his hand, then he'd slap the other shoulder to have that one adjusted. When it came to adjustments, sometimes we had to get creative. Deacon Jones had the flattest feet of anyone I worked with at the Chargers. His arches had fallen so badly that we had to add four extra cleats to each of his shoes to raise his feet off the ground and relieve his pain.

Pat Curran is another interesting story. He came to the Chargers from the Rams. "At the Rams they always gave me two new athletic supporters before each game," he told me. "They had them ready for me in my locker when I came in. They knew I liked to wear two."

Okay, I said to myself. I'll show him how we do it at the Chargers. Before he dressed for the game, I saw him come in and look in his locker. A minute later, he stormed up to the equipment window and said, "Where are my two new athletic supporters?"

"In your locker," I said. "Are you sure you checked for them?"

I went with him to his locker and lifted the *Gameday* magazine and pulled out two new jocks, dyed green. "Two new jocks," I said.

His face reddened. "I'm going to get you for this," he said.

"That's how we do it at the Chargers," I said.

As for jocks, the smallest man on the team wore the biggest jock. But I can't tell you who that was. You'll have to do your own research to figure that one out. Some things in the locker room are meant to stay in the locker room.

Personalities were yet another unique thing to behold. Rickey Young had the most upending, infectious laugh. He came into the locker room laughing and left laughing, leaving everyone laughing in his wake. But not everyone was jovial. Doug Wilkerson was the quietest before a game. And John Jefferson, while very quiet in the locker room and during the pre-game warmups, became a vocal cheerleader at game time. So did Pettis Norman, a soft spoken, kind-hearted, pious man all week long. But on game day, his tongue loosened in his mouth. He walked through the locker room yelling, "Let's go stomp the motherf--kers." After the game he immersed in a tub of ice and returned to the agreeable man he'd been before.

It was hard not to agree with the harmonica playing of Milton Hardaway. He played the harmonica with such soulful harmony that birds came to roost on the fence at our training camp when the harp was in his hands. Also agreeable—to the stomach—was the cooking of Wes Chandler, or "Chef Chandler" as we called him. Wes' hands were as good in the kitchen as they were on the field. He cooked for the team, bringing in shrimp, crawfish, and red beans and rice from New Orleans.

Most players were open to receiving medical treatment for whatever ailed them. But linebacker Woodrow Lowe scorned traditional medicine. He grew up in a small town in Alabama where his grandmother treated his ailments with folk medicine. In one of our games Woody suffered a severe ankle sprain. Upon examination of his ankle, the trainers informed Woody that he'd be unable to practice for several weeks. Woody called his grandmother in Alabama to ask her to send him a poultice of red clay that he could apply to his ankle. To the astonishment of the medical staff and trainers, only two days after applying the red clay poultice, Woodrow was back on the practice field, the swelling in his ankle subsided.

Growing up a boy in the country, Woodrow liked to run barefoot. He ran in the sand along the beaches of San Diego to toughen his feet. One week the team went Anaheim to play the Rams and Woody went out to run in the gravel the baseball team had spread on the field. On his way back in the locker room, Woody spotted a square box filled with sand in the hall outside the locker room. Delighted that someone had been thoughtful enough bring in a box of sand, he jumped in and ran in the gravel for a while, letting it massage his feet while enjoying the feeling of the sand squishing between his toes. Woody was enjoying it so much, he yelled for trainer Jim Hammond. "Hey, Ham-bone," he said, "we should get some of these in San Diego."

Hammond came around the corner to find Woodrow hopping up and down in the box. Hammond slapped his thighs and went to his knees, chortling so hard he almost choked. "Damn, man," Hammond said. "You're marching in cat shit. That's a goddamned kitty litter box."

Woodrow scrambled out of the box and ran to the shower, where he remained for an hour. "Here, kitty, kitty," was all anyone had to say to Woody to get him to put his shoes on.

"Where's my sandbox? Meow," they teased.

14

THE ROAD TO THE BIG SHOW

Getting Revenge Against the Bully

In the 1994 AFC Divisional Playoff game, the Chargers played the Miami Dolphins on January 8, 1995, in Jack Murphy Stadium in San Diego. Bad blood had existed between the Chargers and the Dolphins since that memorable, exhausting playoff game in Miami in 1982. The stakes for this game were high: The winner would face the Steelers at Three Rivers Stadium in Pittsburgh the following week with a trip to the Super Bowl on the line.

It rained on the Thursday before the game. The stadium manager, Bill Wilson, informed the Chargers and the Dolphins that the field would be covered with a tarp to try to keep the playing field dry. The field remained covered all day Friday. Saturday morning, the rain stopped. Bill Wilson advised both teams that it would be wise, in order to protect the game turf, to avoid using the stadium and to instead use the practice field, which was 500 yards southwest of the game field.

The Chargers complied and held a one-hour practice on the practice field at 11 a.m. After practice, the equipment crew went around the practice area to make sure no game plans had been left behind. We went so far as to crumple up fake game plans and throw them in the trash bins. We did that for away games also, knowing the other team would likely check to see if we'd left anything useful behind.

Miami was scheduled to practice at 2 p.m. that day. They dressed for practice in the hotel, and upon arriving at the stadium, they went directly down the entrance to the tunnel where teams entered on game day. The guard stopped them and told them the field was too wet to practice on. He'd been instructed by the stadium manager not to allow anyone on the turf.

One of Miami coach Don Shula's lieutenants got off the bus. "Don Shula has to hold practice on the field where the game is going to be played," he told the guard.

"I can't let you do that," the guard responded.

"Do you know who Don Shula is?" the lieutenant asked.

"I do," the guard said.

"Well, stand aside and let his team on the field," the lieutenant demanded.

The guard stood back, clearing the way for the team. The tarp had been removed to allow the field to dry, but it was still so soggy the water and mud came up to the tops of players' shoes. Shula had a torn Achilles' tendon at the time and couldn't walk. He came off the bus on a motorized cart, which he drove all over the mushy turf while conducting practice, leaving deep tracks in the field. Those of us with the Chargers who had anything to do with the field and its preparation were quite ticked off at Shula for bullying his way around and disregarding our orders.

The weather forecast called for slight rain again Saturday night and Sunday morning, so the grounds crew covered the field again after the Dolphins' practice. The rain came as predicted, and didn't really let up until late Sunday morning. On game day, I arrived at the stadium at 5:30 a.m., my usual time, and was greeted by the smell of bacon frying in a pan.

The scent drifted out from the training room. Keoki Kamau, the head trainer at the time, cooked breakfast for the dungeon rats on Sunday mornings before home games.

"Guess what?" said Keoki.

"What?" I asked.

"Someone didn't like Don Shula's attitude and got into the visiting team's locker room last night and unplugged all the quarterback's communication radios they left charging for the game," he told me. "And if that wasn't enough, they put Don Shula's cart up on blocks and left it running all night."

"No kidding?"

"Yes, but the damned thing didn't run out of gas like they hoped. They should have emptied the tank," Keoki surmised.

"I don't know how anyone could have gotten in there," I said. "I saw Bobby Monica, the Dolphins' equipment manager, lock the door with his key."

"Well, don't worry. Whoever it was got back in this morning and plugged the radios in and took the cart down off the blocks." Keoki laughed.

I was truly surprised. I had done some things to make life tough for the Dolphins in our territory, but even I hadn't thought of anything like that. Before pregame warmups, Shula sent for me. I knew he'd found out about the break in, but that wasn't what he wanted to discuss. He had another complaint. A small office—no bigger than a large closet—was located inside the visiting team locker room, serving as a dressing room for the ball boys and the chain crew. Shula screamed, "I want them out of here," and pointed to the ball boys.

I just looked at him as if he were a mad man and turned and walked away. I didn't say anything to the ball boys. That room had been reserved for them, and that's where they stayed. I didn't look back, leaving Shula in a furious state.

Later, during pregame warmups, Shula was back at it, scooting his motorized cart all over the field, creating large track marks in the turf before the game. Bill Wilson fumed, muttering how dumb an act it was. He wanted the grounds in good condition for the important game.

"It doesn't make sense to me," Bill said, shaking his head in annoyance. "Seems to me like he's just not thinking."

That's the truth: Shula wasn't thinking about anyone but himself. No one could tell Don Shula what to do, but make no mistake about it—he was digging his team's grave.

At halftime, the Chargers trailed the Dolphins, 21-6. Stan Brock, the Chargers' 6 foot, 6 inch, 295-pound tackle, slammed his helmet into the wall of the visiting team locker room as he stormed up the tunnel. His attack on the stadium wall inadvertently hit one of the two electrical boxes in the hallway and blew the lights out in the Dolphins locker room, but Stan didn't know that. When the Dolphin players got to the locker room, they found themselves in the dark.

Bobby Monica, the equipment manager, asked the visiting team assistant, who happened to be my son, Joe, to find a maintenance man to get the lights back on. Joe sprinted down the hall into a larger part of the stadium basement, out of sight of the Dolphins locker room. He stood there, snickering, and proceeded to count his fingers and his toes. He spent a few more minutes counting the beams in the ceiling. When he figured he had used up a significant amount of the halftime break, he headed back to the Dolphins locker room, pretending to be out of breath as though his mad hunt for help had almost done him in. He reported to Monica that he couldn't find a maintenance crew member anywhere.

Meanwhile, Shula was blowing off steam like a heated locomotive. The offense moved to the dimly lit, tiny room the ball boys and chain crew dressed in, a room barely big enough for six ball boys and six crew men. By the time the blackboard had been moved into the room, not all of the players would fit. The Miami defense held its meeting in the hall—"just sitting in the dark," Dolphins safety, Michael Stewart, said at the time.

Meanwhile, none of us had any knowledge that Stan Brock's act of frustration had put Miami in the dark. We found out the following day, when Shula blamed me for turning the lights out on them. I was always hospitable to all visiting teams, providing the assistance they needed as our guests in San Diego. I believed the game should be won on the field, and sometimes with a little help from friends. I had nothing to do with them being in the dark, but the lights going out was the least of the Dolphins' worries that day.

The Chargers' resurgence in the second half began when the Chargers' Reuben Davis stopped the Dolphins' Bernie Parmalee in the end zone for a safety to make the score 21-8. Then on a long drive by the Chargers, running back Natrone Means broke several tackles on a 24-yard run to score a touchdown, trimming the Dolphins' lead to 21-15. Later in the fourth quarter, Chargers quarterback Stan Humphries hit Mark Seay for the go-ahead touchdown, giving San Diego a one-point lead, 22-21.

With 35 seconds left in the game, Miami—who had not yet scored in the second half—had the ball on the Chargers' 30-yard line. Miami's field goal kicker, Pete Stoyanovich, positioned himself in front of the ball for a 48-yard field goal attempt. The crowd went silent. The outcome of the game— and the rest of the season—hinged on the kick. The holder squatted. He had no choice but to place the ball in one of the muddy trenches left on the field by Shula's cart. Pete kicked. The clock ticked. The ball sputtered in the mud of one of the tire ruts and fell short of the goal line. Chargers fans leaped to their feet, while Shula gunned his cart off the field in the midst of the happy roar of the San Diego crowd. The Chargers were on their way to play Pittsburgh for the chance to play in the Super Bowl.

The next day, Steve Shaushan, the stadium operator, said his employees weren't notified of any problems in the locker room during the game with the lights. To this day, Don Shula insists that I turned the lights out on them.

A Good Night's Rest, at Last

A buzz engulfed Pittsburgh in the days leading up to our game with them. Banners flew throughout the city proclaiming the Steelers as Miami bound (where the Super Bowl was to be played). My family had come along on the trip, and we held our hope inside, milling quietly among the celebrants, lest we jinx our chance of victory. During mass the night before the game, Monsignors I. Brent Eagan and Dan Dillabough, two of our team chaplains, asked the higher power to tip the scales in our favor—not for ourselves, of course, but for the city of San Diego.

Of all the tricks I'd played on teams visiting the Chargers, none compared to the horrors the citizens of Pittsburgh put us through the night before the game. Outside our hotel, dogs barked and howled every hour on the hour. Sirens hurled their screams in close proximity with regularity. The heat in the hotel where the team was housed reached an unbearable level, and the hotel's engineers said they couldn't fix it until morning. Used to the cool nights in Southern California, all of us from San Diego were worn and haggard the next morning after a near-sleepless night. A light rain fell on Sunday morning, and when I awoke to it, my heart did a war dance inside my chest as adrenaline pumped through my body. Leaving the hotel that morning, we put our best face forward, trying to appear bright and rested. We didn't dare let Pittsburgh fans know that they had gotten to us.

As kick-off neared, I cheered loudly for my team. The game got underway with Steelers' fans waving their bright yellow "terrible towels." The outnumbered Chargers' fans presented a sprinkling of blue among the black and yellow. As the game began, the Chargers seemed to be standing still. The Steelers outgained them in total yards 229 to 46 in the first half and led 10-3 at halftime. I had a sinking feeling in my stomach, remembering the championship game in Cincinnati in January of 1982, when the Chargers failed to get their motor going.

During halftime, coach Bobby Ross didn't single anyone out, but addressed the whole team in discussing missing assignments. But among the players, I overheard a rallying cry: "We've got to show up!"

After the half, Pittsburgh struck first with a field goal, and it looked as if the Chargers were going to lose by a big spread. But then Stan Humphries connected with Al Pupunu on a 43-yard touchdown to trim the gap to 13-10. Neither team scored again until late in the fourth quarter when Stan threw another 43-yard touchdown pass, this time to Tony Martin, to give the Chargers a 17-13 lead.

I held my breath as the seconds ticked away in the last quarter of the AFC championship game. With the Chargers leading by four points, it was fourth down for the Steelers with one minute and four seconds left on the clock. As he usually did in a tight game, Stan Humphries stood next to me with his arm around my shoulder. By this time in my career, I was thought of as a father figure, someone to lean on.

The Steelers had the ball in scoring range, and it appeared they would score a touchdown to win—at least they thought they would. So too did NFL Properties, who had delivered the AFC Championship caps and shirts to the Steelers' locker-room door. But on both counts, the gun was jumped. Steelers quarterback Neil O'Donnell released his pass. Receiver Barry Foster raced across the center of the field directly in the path of the oncoming pass. The ball curved and dived toward the waiting hands of Foster near the end zone, but just as he was about to grab the winning touchdown, the Chargers' Dennis Gibson rose into the air and swatted down the pass. Time ran out, and we were going to the Super Bowl.

I stood on the sideline at Three Rivers Stadium stunned, holding my breath as our win over the Steelers sunk in. The Pittsburgh sideline appeared sullen, their fans in a state of shock. Then slowly, the fans sunk back into their seats. Meanwhile, Stan was hugging me. The Chargers on the field began dancing and jumping for joy, some with tears in their eyes as

I had in mine. All around me the trickling of Chargers fans throughout the stadium worked themselves into a frenzy.

I searched the stands for my family, and saw them scream- ing, hugging, laughing, and crying. The reality of our situation hit me with a wave of happiness that was dizzying. I had waited 23 years for this day. Even though I had only dressed them, I felt that I had helped them along, possibly given them some edge that worked to their advantage. As much as this victory belonged to them, their victory also belonged to me.

When I turned back to the field, some of the Steelers players were still on the bench, their heads lowered into their hands, the grievous actualization of defeat seemingly too tax- ing to bear. One of their players, Tim McKyer, the Pittsburgh defender who'd been covering Tony Martin when he caught the winning touchdown, had collapsed to the ground and was being helped up. I remembered that feeling from the year we'd left our chance to play in the big game in the cold of Cincin- nati, and I felt for them.

I flew back to San Diego with the team that night, and my wife stayed over in Pittsburgh. She said the hotel was a com- fortable 68 degrees that evening. No barking dogs, no sirens screaming outside, and no Steelers headed to the Super Bowl. She enjoyed a good night's rest—as did the rest of the team.

The Big Game

I had waited my entire career for the big game. I wanted to share the joy with all of the talented players who had played for the Chargers during my career, and had not had the chance to experience the Super Bowl. After our win in Pittsburgh, the city of San Diego went bonkers. A huge crowd of fans waited for us at the stadium when we returned to town. The attention was spectacular, but we had less than a week to prepare for the trip to Miami.

Monday was a regular practice day for the team, and Tuesday was the players' day off. But the guys were so fired up that most of them came in on their own without the coaches around and worked out intently, lifting weights and watching tapes of the San Francisco 49ers, our opponent in the Super Bowl. I had never witnessed that kind of dedication from the team before any other game.

I was allotted 21 tickets by general manager Bobby Beathard—who really took care of me—so I packed up my entire family and took them along to Miami. Stan Humphries gave me two of his tickets on the Chargers' charter plane to use for my family. The treatment we received from the Super Bowl committee and the league far exceeded my expectations. The whole experience was like a fairy tale.

Ending up in Miami after beating the Dolphins on the way to Super Bowl was quite ironic. On our first day of practice upon arriving in Miami, we encountered Dolphins players who were still cleaning out their lockers. I imagined that they were feeling like they should have been the ones preparing for another game. The so-called bad blood between us continued.

Although the Dolphins were hospitable, Don Shula saw Joe Green and me playing dominoes. He passed us and said to Joe, "Kick his ass." I had still never been formally introduced to the man, despite the fact that he had already barked at me in San Diego. I just laughed in response.

Don Shula aside, most things went smoothly at the Super Bowl. I had always been an innovator, and I had Super Bowl logos sewn on the players' jerseys—a first at that time. The league informed me that I couldn't dress the players in those jerseys for the game because of the addition of the logo. I was always prepared and had brought along spares. So I said we wouldn't wear them in the game, but the players still wore them in the team picture. The following year the league made it mandatory for the teams in the Super Bowl to wear the logos on their jerseys. Go figure.

The league also sent us specific shoes for the players to wear. They were baseball shoes made to look like football shoes, and emblazoned with the words "Big Hurt" on them.

Everyone knows who he was—Chicago White Sox slugger Frank Thomas. I called the league and told them that we could not wear those shoes. I left the equipment room for a while and when I got back in the locker room, the shoe rep was showing the players the shoes.

"You can't do that," I told him. I called Bobby Beathard and told him about the situation. Two hours later, Bill Hampton, who was from the league office, came down to the locker room. "I have been told to make you happy," he said. I don't know if he was being sarcastic, but I do know the Chargers didn't wear those shoes.

Our players were like children on the night before Christmas, starry-eyed and high with anticipation. Security was tight during our stay, and bed check was enforced with warden-like scrutiny. In the locker room before the game, the team was tense, but no more so than before any other big game. Then the referee knocked on the door and told us, "It's time to go." Our players couldn't get past their awe, their eyes suddenly as wide as buckets.

I imagine it was hard for them to stop being a spectator in all the glamour of the festive event. Before we knew it, the 49ers had slam-dunked us. By halftime, we were down 28-10. I knew we were out of the game when Stan Humphries failed to come and stand beside me with his arm around my shoulder as usual. It didn't change the fact that we were there, and the experience will last a lifetime.

Chargers defensive lineman Blaise Winter watched the play from the sideline. Two years earlier the Chargers had lost a playoff game to Miami in that same stadium. Inside the Chargers' locker room that day the silence was deafening, as if the world had stopped being. Blaise, who had begged his way back into the NFL, told his teammates that day, "We're going to finish this. I know we will, and I'm going to be a part of it. We're going to play in the Super Bowl."

Standing on the field two years later prior to the start of the Super Bowl, Blaise was in tears. The starters came on to the field in uniform, but Blaise was not with them. He'd blown his knee out and couldn't play in the big game. But he was with the team in spirit, along with so many Chargers who had come before him.

But on this day, San Diego just didn't have what it took to win the game. San Francisco continued its offensive onslaught in the second half, tacking on three more touchdowns on their way to a 49-26 drubbing. The result wasn't favorable, but just having been to the Super Bowl was a great accomplishment—one that I will never forget.

15

MY LAST YEAR

When I announced to the front office that I'd be leaving the team in April of 2000, I didn't expect the joy ride that awaited me during my last year with the Chargers. The team advised the media through a press release that I'd be leaving at the end of the season, and I was flooded with interview requests. I had good rapport with the press, and I was happy to talk with them. Most of them had been around over the years through all my blunders and knew me well.

During my last training camp, I got a big lift from the players on the go-karts which they rode back and forth from the dorms to the practice field, and to the dining hall. I'd always received special treatment from the players, but in my final training camp, they took extra special care of me and always made sure that there was an empty seat in one of their go-karts. In addition to transporting me around, they also brought me food, cookies, and soft drinks.

When the season started, every team we played provided me with some kind of tribute to my career. For my last home game against the Raiders, the players made me the honorary team captain, which meant that I got to run out of the tunnel with the team. The Chargers gave me a five-minute tribute on the scoreboard prior to the game, showing highlights from my 27-year career. Then Junior Seau and Vaughn Parker escorted me to the center of the field for the coin toss.

"You'd better not drop a tear," Junior joked with me. Vaughn looked straight ahead, and Junior developed a sudden case of hay fever. I called heads, and the referee flipped the coin. Heads won, and the Raiders' team captain, Tim Brown, and the other Raiders wished me well.

My last game with the Chargers was a road match against the Broncos in Denver. Junior Seau was on the injured list and didn't make the trip with the team. We always had dinner together the night before a game. So he flew on his own to Denver to make sure that we wouldn't miss our last dinner together. He treated all the trainers and equipment crew to dinner for my last farewell. I was named team captain again, and once again I won the coin toss with a guess of heads. Denver gave me a tribute on the scoreboard, too, and when the game ended, Junior Seau walked off the field with me for the last time.

Coach Mike Shanahan, whom I've always had special regard for, wished me a great retirement, offered me tickets to a Broncos game whenever I wished, and gave me a game ball from the Broncos. For the record, we never played any tricks on them, or any team in our division.

The whirlwind year was topped off with a trip to the Pro Bowl as a guest of the NFL, where I was honorary equipment man for the NFC.

The Chargers said I could retire a bit earlier than planned if I wished, and so I gladly accepted their offer. On my actual last day, I drove my car to the facility on Murphy Canyon Road and parked it out front. I said goodbye to some folks and left through the front door.

The San Diego Chargers and the NFL are a long way from Saint Genevieve, Missouri, where I grew up with my father and two brothers in a section of that historical town aptly named Mud Town. Every day I worked for the Chargers was a blessing that I'm humbly thankful for. A quote I learned from Dan Henning speaks to the way I tried to spend my NFL career: "Expect nothing. Blame no one. Get the job done." I did my job with a love for all of the people I was privileged to share my experience with around the league. I did it my way, and if I had it to do over again, I wouldn't change a thing.

Epilogue

The locker room in this book exists in reality the same as the bridges in *The Bridges of Madison County*, but according to the equipment men around the league, unlike the bridges, that locker room that once was, no longer exists. True, the construction is the same, the lockers stand in the ready, and football players pass through on their way to practices and games. But the locker room has changed into a place where eyes meet with a glance, and greetings are made in passing. iPads, iPhones, and electronic games with ear phones blocking out the world have replaced the boom boxes, the coffee and doughnuts, the camaraderie, the domino games, and the tricks played on one another. In the Sid Brooks era, players got drafted into a football team family. Some were likely to stay with a team until they retired, as many of the players did during Sid's tenure. Dan Fouts and Sid were rookies together, and when Dan left the Chargers he had played for his one and only professional football team. When a player was cut or traded, his teammates felt as if they'd lost a family member. There would be sadness until they welcomed the newest member. But these days, equipment managers say players are more in touch with their iPhones and agents than they are with their teammates. Football is a business, and businesses have to change with the times in order to survive; that is understandable. Much of the electronic obsession in the locker room subsists because the coaches in the league now are from the same generation as the players. This may not be at all bad, but the good old days that Sid brought to the locker room are gone forever.

Sid retired from the Chargers in April, 2000. The league was beginning to change, and he felt it coming. His ability to run the locker room his way was becoming a challenge. He wanted to always remember his locker room the way it had been, and packing tons of equipment for the road is a young man's job. Sid said, "I'll always love football, but I just kind of sat back and looked at the fact that I cannot beat a rookie in the 40-yard dash anymore."

When he left the Chargers he addressed the team. These are his parting words:

"I want you all to know how much the opportunity to be a part of this team and to share the National Championship with you means to me. Your youth, enthusiasm, and commitment to excellence have rejuvenated these old bones so much so that my spirit has been elevated to your youthfulness. I'll be as proud as any parent watching your future play. I've been on a joy ride. Thank you, Sid."

Sid "The Doc" died Friday April 13, 2007.

—Gerri Brooks, 2014

Acknowledgments

I was blessed with a wonderful career, and for that I must thank some kind folks. I'm deeply appreciative to my friend, Harold Lewis; my co-passengers in the cabs to the stadiums for many years—Dan Fouts, Kellen Winslow, and Charlie Joiner; and the stadium board for the plaque that bears my name and is placed in the locker room at Qualcomm Stadium.

Many thanks to my loyal assistants, Bronco Hinek and Bob Wick; to all the ball boys—including my sons, Joe, Michael, and Brett—who contributed to the early graying of my hair; to Karen Hudson, who helped me in so many ways; to my good friend, Ernie Zampese; to all the players who refreshed my memory with their stories; and most of all to my wife, Gerri. Without her help, this book would not have been written.

I am honored to have had the privilege of working alongside five general managers: Harland Svare, the late Johnny Sanders, Ron Nay, Steve Ortmayer, and Bobby Beathard, whom I'm especially grateful to for allowing me to represent the Chargers at the NFL draft each of my last ten years, and for his lasting friendship. Special thanks to the ten Chargers' head coaches of my career—Harland Svare, Ron Waller, the late Tommy Prothro, Don Coryell, Al Saunders, Dan Henning, Bobby Ross, Kevin Gilbride, June Jones, and Mike Riley—and to all the assistant coaches and players who crossed the threshold of the locker room, made my career a fun-filled journey, and left me with their life-long brotherhood.